# Fresh Light

Homilies
on the
Gospels of
Year B

# Fresh Light

Homilies on the Gospels of Year B

Joseph Pollard

**Hillenbrand**Books

Chicago / Mundelein, Illinois

*First published in the UK by The Columba Press/55A Spruce
Avenue Stillorgan Industrial Park /Blackrock Co., Dublin/Ireland.*
UK edition © 2002 Joseph Pollard. Published by arrangement
with the author and publisher.

FRESH LIGHT: HOMILIES ON THE GOSPELS OF YEAR B / NORTH
AMERICAN EDITION © 2005 Archdiocese of Chicago: Liturgy Training
Publications, 1800 North Hermitage Avenue, Chicago IL 60622-1101;
1-800-933-1800, fax 1-800-933-7094, e-mail orders@ltp.org. All rights
reserved. See our website at www.ltp.org.

**Hillenbrand Books** is an imprint of Liturgy Training Publications (LTP) and
the Liturgical Institute at the University of Saint Mary of the Lake (USML).
The imprint is focused on contemporary and classical theological thought
concerning the liturgy of the Catholic Church. Available at bookstores everywhere, or through LTP by calling 1-800-933-1800 or visiting www.ltp.org.
Further information about the **Hillenbrand Books** publishing program is
available from the University of Saint Mary of the Lake/Mundelein Seminary,
1000 East Maple Avenue, Mundelein, IL 60060 (847-837-4542), on the
web at www.usml.edu/liturgicalinstitute, or e-mail litinst@usml.edu.

Printed in the United States of America.

Library of Congress Control Number: 2005929593

ISBN 1-59525-012-3

HFFLB

"Above all, it's the Gospels that occupy my mind. I'm always finding fresh light there."

Thérèse of Lisieux, *Story of a Soul, The Autobiography of St. Therese of Lisieux*

# Contents

**Solemnities and Feasts of the Lord and Saints**

For Martin Sheen

*Who helps God keep
his promises to the poor*

# Introduction

The homilies in this volume of *Fresh Light* are short, and are based on the Gospels for the Sundays of Year B. Like the first volume of *Fresh Light*, homilies for some solemnities and feasts are also included. I've added textual explication, but have kept it to a minimum in order to concentrate on applying the Gospel message to the pastoral circumstances of our time.

One dimension of this book is to think of these homilies as a catechesis based on the word of God, which I believe is needed for our time and culture. It is a time described by one observer as "theologically unraveling" and a culture described as "unmoored." These homilies, consequently, place Jesus "front and center" (and without apology) as Savior and Lord. They support our people's faith and trust in him at this time.

Hope is another dimension of this book. I trust that the reader will find in these homilies "the assurance of hope" (Hebrews 6:11) that accompanies us on the road of life, and a strong sense of "the hope reserved for you in heaven" (Colossians 1:5) that completes our faith journey. Homilies are always in the business of affirming the hope of Christ that is already present in people's hearts.

One such journey is documented by Paulo Coelho, the author of *The Pilgrimage* (San Francisco: HarperSanFrancisco, 1995). It is an account of his journey along the medieval pilgrim route to Santiago de Compostela. While on his journey, he soon learns that he is not walking the road, but that the road is "walking" him. He learns the inverted lesson of life's road: we do not impose our teaching on the road, but find the road teaching us. The same discovery was made by the disciples on the road to Emmaus. They came to understand their confused lives through what and who the road surprisingly unfolded before them.

For you and I, the Gospel is the pilgrim route chosen as followers of our Lord. It is our road through life. We impose nothing on it. It speaks to us. It shows us the way.

# Advent

# 2b First Sunday of Advent

## Mark 13:33–37

### Watching as We Wait

In today's Gospel, our Lord is talking about what is popularly called "the second coming," his coming again at the end of time. He wants us to watch for it. He wants us to be prepared to meet him. The second coming is an event that will occur in history. It may happen in our lifetime. Should we die before the time, then the coming will take the form of Jesus meeting us at the hour of our death. Either way, Jesus wants us to be ready.

A parishioner said to me one Sunday after Mass: "If you priests knew how some young people unwind on the weekends, you'd know why they're missing from Mass on Saturday evenings and Sunday mornings. They're not in any shape to attend."

Well, that's not exactly news to the men in any rectory. Some people unwind unwisely on the weekends and after work. Alcohol is a big part of our culture of relaxation, and increasingly so among the young. Not, indeed, that alcohol has no competition from drugs and other mindless pursuits! All of them help to depress their users, and they contribute to the long roll call of personal psychological difficulties, domestic abuse—and non-attendance at church.

When Jesus comes on the final day and says, "Last call, gentlemen!" I hope it will not be a Saturday or a Sunday because it's not just some in our community who may not be ready to meet him; it's also a lot of the over-pampered Western world. There is such a frenzy to their weekends and to their drinking and their drug taking! What are they in such hot pursuit of? The same parishioner answered that question for me: "Oblivion," he said. Therefore, it seems that the Bible's preference for the poor will apply on the last day as it has throughout salvation history: only the poor, the *anawim*, the little ones, the friends of God, will be ready to meet him. They haven't the money or the heart to support such drunken and drugged distraction.

Jesus says, "You do not know when the lord of the house is coming. . . . Watch!" You and I are here at Mass this morning, not at home coping with a hangover. Sure, we enjoy our glass or two, and we enjoy the good things of life.

That is as it should be. For we follow a Lord who ate and drank at wedding feasts and at religious festivals, and with sinners as well as saints. But we are not wedded to the pleasures of life as so many of our contemporaries appear to be. We balance the pleasures of the outer life with the joys of the inner life; with having a real relationship with Jesus; with knowing his peace in our hearts; with evaluating pleasures and reading the map of life by his moral compass; with knowing how to cast our cares and our losses on him; with looking forward with firm hope to the future; with not being caught unawares; with not being alarmed should he come among us even now and say, "It's last call, dear friend!" For we are his friends, and the friends of God have no fear.

Our Lord is coming, and the final day is drawing near. It is important that we do not weaken and exchange what we have for the illusions others only suffer under. I speak to the younger people among us particularly, and my only desire is to spare them illusion and the loss of their best years.

Carlo Carretto, in his book *In Search of the Beyond* (New York: Doubleday, 1978), cites a proverb of the Taureg tribes of North Africa: "Place the tents far apart: draw near with your hearts." We should place the tents of illusion far apart from us and draw our hearts ever nearer to the word of God. We should continue to distance ourselves from our culture's high-density swirl, from the boozed voices "full of sound and fury" and the drugged voices "signifying nothing"—to use Shakespeare's words (Macbeth, V)—of any value to the spiritual journey. The very young may be tempted to feel that there must be some form of divine ecstasy in all this buzz, but by Monday morning it is clear enough that there is nothing at all in the buzz, and that a fair percentage of society is hungover for want of listening to its God and half-blind from the shimmering weekend mirages that steal the place of his shining face.

Jesus says, "What I say to you, I say to all: 'Watch!'" Those of us will, for whom the Lord's coming has nothing to do with illusion and oblivion and everything to do with the hope of glory.

# 5B Second Sunday of Advent

## MARK 1:1–8

### The Only Highway that Matters

It's that time of year again when all of us start preparing. We are preparing for Christmas. For many people, preparing for Christmas is not the huge labor of love that it ought to be, but a huge exasperation.

Why is that? Well, there are obligations of all sorts to be met at this time of year. There are Christmas cards to be sent, especially the ones that our conscience says must be accompanied by the annual letter. There's a whole family to be decked-out for Christmas, seasonably and therefore expensively. There are gifts to be bought. There are parties to be prepared. There are old enmities to be glossed over for business reasons as the spouse invites his or her business contacts over for a cup of Christmas cheer. There are uncomfortable in-laws to be greeted for the sake of your better half.

There are carolers collecting at the door, the Salvation Army collecting at the mall, and a rush of begging letters from all the charities in the world. Then there's the religious aspect—a Mass seat to be found among all the strangers suddenly showing up in church! The trappings of Christmas have come to overlay the feast—and half-murder our hearts in the process. As essayist E. B. White reminds us in his timeless classic, *The Second Tree from the Corner* (New York: Harper & Row, 1984), "To perceive Christmas through its wrapping becomes more difficult with every year."

In contrast to all of that are the words of John the Baptist. He is the herald's voice from the book of the prophet Isaiah, crying: "Prepare the way of the LORD, make straight his paths." That is what preparing for Christmas is really all about. It's about getting ourselves ready for the Savior to be born in our hearts and, beyond Christmas, getting ready for the final coming of Christ when all the trappings and the wrappings of our lives are drawn down.

Over the past seventy years or so, transportation authorities in many countries have been busy building great interstate highways, freeways, and motorways. In this way, they have connected their nations' hinterlands with their cities and seaports and airports. They have been, at one and the same time, unifying their nations and facilitating business and commerce. In the process, some hills are flattened, some depressions filled in, and some structures removed.

What the mechanical diggers and the earthmovers do is paralleled spiritually in the follow-on words of John the Baptist, (as given in Luke's Gospel): "Every valley shall be filled / And every mountain and hill / shall be made low. / The winding roads shall be made straight / And the rough ways made smooth" (Luke 3:5). These lines tell us how we may prepare for Christmas by telling us how to prepare the way of the Lord. We are to level the hills of our sins and fill in the valleys of our failures and omissions. We are to make smooth the rough ways of our incivility and our lack of graciousness toward others. We are to create the most important road of all—a highway for our God. It is the only highway that matters in the long run, the road by which God can come straight into our open-gated hearts at Christmas and at life's end.

We cannot avoid a certain amount of distraction as we prepare for Christmas. We cannot ignore all of the time-tested Christmas traditions, nor should we discard the entire legacy that past generations have placed on our yuletide shoulders. On the other hand, we cannot afford to be swamped by too many externals, aggravated by the myriad social obligations, and choked by the commercial paraphernalia of the feast. All of these things have practically derailed God and have almost lost for Christmas its true meaning and its genuine spirit. Maybe it's time to start cutting back on some of this packaging, and maybe it's time to start unfolding the true meaning and the priceless Gift again.

Prepare the way for your Lord first. Prepare your heart for his birth in it at Christmas. Otherwise, this saving event is robbed of meaning for you in time and in eternity. Let whatever else you do in preparation for Christmas be only the expression of your renewed and grateful heart.

# 8B Third Sunday of Advent

## JOHN 1:6–8, 19–28

### The Witness

In one of Sergio Leone's old spaghetti westerns from 1968, "Once Upon a Time in the West," known for their generosity of slow-motion blood and piles of corpses, Henry Fonda keeps asking Charles Bronson, "Who are you?" And vagabond Bronson keeps answering with a few eerie notes on his harmonica. The question "Who are you?" is incidental at first. Later, it becomes a matter of urgency. Fonda senses a personal threat, something out of his past maybe. But he never gets his answer until it is too late. Too bad for him. By movie's end, Fonda is added to the generous heap of corpses.

In today's Gospel, the priests and Levites ask John the Baptist, "Who are you?" It is not an incidental question. There is urgency and persistence in their questioning of John. The Jewish authorities, who sent them out into the desert to ask the question, feel threatened. John is preparing the way for the Lord, for the messiah, and the authorities are having none of it. Their logic is simple. Since they are the official religious authority, surely it is to them and not to John that God will reveal the coming of the messiah, and surely it is they who own the right to announce his appearance when he comes. God owes it to their religious authority!

And so, the messengers ask, "Who are you?" John answers, "I am not the messiah." John, fed on locusts and wild honey, certainly doesn't look like anybody's messiah. Most people were expecting a messiah who would be an imposing son of David, who would lead them to victory over the Romans, and who would establish a great political kingdom on the earth. John looks more like a vagabond.

"What are you then? Are you Elijah?" they ask him. The prophet Malachi, some 500 years previously, spoke of the coming of the messiah in a particular way. He spoke of it, somewhat perilously, when "the day of the LORD comes, the great and terrible day (Malachi 3:24). He said that the messiah would be preceded by Elijah. Elijah would first come to prepare the messiah's way. It is with these perilous words—"the great and terrible day"—that the Jewish Old Testament ends. (Scholars suggest that the softening sentence, "Lo, I will send you Elijah . . . before the day . . . to turn the hearts of the fathers to their children and the hearts of the children to their fathers" [vv. 23–24] was added later because Judaism did not want its holy scriptures to end on a threatening note.) John answers, "No. [I am not Elijah]."

"Are you the prophet?" they ask next. In the context of the coming of the messiah, it was believed that "the prophet" (either Isaiah or Jeremiah, there being two traditions) would also return with the messiah and with Elijah. Isaiah was the more favored as the prophet of the return. John answers that he is not the prophet.

"Who are you," they ask, "so we can give an answer to those who sent us?" John answers, quoting the words of the prophet Isaiah: "I am 'the voice of one crying out in the desert, / 'Make straight the way of the Lord.'"

Theologian William Barclay tells us, in his commentary *The Gospel of John: The New Daily Study Bible* (Nashville, TN: Westminster John Knox Press, 2001), that the roads of the Middle East were not as our roads are: they were no more than paths or tracks. When a king was about to visit a province, and when a conqueror was about to travel through his domains, the roads were smoothed and straightened out. John is preparing the spiritual road for the messiah, a smooth and level and straight road, so that the messiah may travel all the more easily into the waiting hearts of his people.

John the Baptist prepared the Lord's way in his own time and place. He gave witness to his generation that Jesus was the Messiah, and that the age of salvation had arrived. We, too, are the beneficiaries of John's witnessing, a witnessing that eventually cost him his life. As we prepare for Christmas, the plea of John must be in front of our faces. Every other Christmas consideration is only a poor second in the Baptist's book. We, too, are making a "straight way" for the Lord into our hearts. For any Christian, this is the first order of Christmas business and its core concern.

# 11B Fourth Sunday of Advent

## LUKE 1:26–38

### Let It Be

Do you remember the Beatles (Paul McCartney's "other group")?
I was too old to hitch my heart to the Beatles' bandwagon when it
came along. And I was too experienced to buy into much of the Beatles'
philosophy of life. But that didn't blind me to the basic idealism of the
group as they choreographed their particular vision of a better world
and begged us, in one soft-sell musical mantra, to just "Let It Be."

The word *amen* is a word that means "let it be." It is one of
the words most frequently on our lips. We say it over and over at the
liturgy and in private prayer. I myself seldom think of what I'm saying
when I say it. For most of us, amen is just a sort of period to whatever
it is that went before.

The Oxford Dictionary of the Bible tells me that *amen* is the
Hebrew word for certainly, I agree, let-it-be. It tells me that *amen*
was an everyday expression that found its way into Hebrew liturgical
life. Our own liturgy is heir to Hebrew liturgical language, and so we
finish each Christian prayer by stating our consent to it: we say amen,
certainly, I agree, let-it-be. Mary said let-it-be to the angel's invitation and to God's will. And because of her let-it-be we have something
called Christmas to celebrate.

Mary is our great model of the amen. Anything she said amen
to became a reality in her life. She did not give notional assent to
God's will, but real assent. She did not discern God's will for her life
and then start questioning its whys and wherefores. His will came
to be in her simply because she let it be. Some people call this "obedience to God's will." I prefer Saint Josemaría Escrivá's view of it as
"correspondence to grace" *(Christ is Passing By)*.

The secret of a happy life is correspondence to grace.
Correspondence to grace means uncovering God's will day-by-day
as best we can and corresponding with that will as best we understand it. In that way, we move with God's impulses rather than our

own. There is no other way by which the definition of the Christian as a servant of God can become a reality in our lives.

Mary said, "I am the handmaid of the Lord. Let it be done to me according to your word." When she said that, God's saving plan for us was able to enter its critical phase. For Mary's let-it-be determined where the human nature of the Savior would come from. It would come from Mary. All of us became beneficiaries of Mary's let-it-be. She herself came to know the joy of doing the right thing, in the right place, at the right time. Isn't doing the right thing, in the right place, at the right time the goal of practical wisdom? It is also the meaning of doing God's will in your life.

Mary's amen was the right thing, in the right place, at the right time both for our salvation and for her own personal history. There is a similar rightness of action, place, and time in our amens to the will of God, less momentous though they be, both in regard to our personal histories and in regard to the wider, mysterious connections of God's saving plan for others through us.

Uncovering God's will for us is critical to the experience of religion as a personal relationship with God. Lacking this fundamental connection with God in the alignment of our will with the divine will, everything is fits-and-starts with us and, ultimately, discouragement and disappointment. Maybe this is why some of us experience life in God no deeper than the outer forms of religion, and why we do not live out our days at the deeper level where one will harmonize with the other.

When we live the correspondence of wills on a daily basis, we experience the presence of God and the assurance of salvation in a way that eludes us in the outer forms of religion, and we come to know in our hearts what Saint Paul called "the peace of God that surpasses all understanding" (Philemon 4:7).

Living our life as God wills it for us has nothing to do with being a slave or with abandoning our intelligence and our conscience. It has to do with the royal road of freedom. It has to do with Christian maturity. It has to do with attaining "the full stature of Christ" (Ephesians 4:13). Jesus followed God's will perfectly, and yet did so in perfect freedom. His death for us was a charge he had from the Father and, at the same time, it was a matter of freely laying down his life and taking it up again freely: "I lay down my life in order to take it up again. No one takes it from me, but I lay it down on my own. I have power to lay it down, and power to take it up again" (John 10:17–18).

God's will does not enslave us: it allows us to be servants of the word as Mary was. It is in serving this word (understood here as God's will) day by day and action by action that the freedom we most desire is actually realized. We do not abandon our intellect in following God's will but use it at its most discovering level. Nor do we by-pass conscience in following God's will but find conscience's deepest inclinations moving us, in full freedom, into the way of God's disclosure. To do God's will is, ultimately, to discover and to do my own deepest and most gracious desires.

# Christmas

# 13ABC The Nativity of the Lord

**December 24 / At the Vigil Mass**

## MATTHEW 1:1–25 (LONGER) OR MATTHEW 1:18–25 (SHORTER)

**Joy to the World!**

Joy to the world: the Lord is near! On this eve of our dear Savior's birth, I wish you a joyful Christmas!

The Gospel proclamation, which we have just heard, is part of St. Matthew's introduction to the wonderful story of Christmas. It gives us some wonderful insights into the child that was born on that first Christmas night. It is these insights that allow us to announce joy to the world.

Our Gospel reading highlights three things. The first is the role of the Holy Spirit in the birth of the child of Christmas. The second is the name that Joseph is told to give the child, the name *Jesus*. The third is the name Matthew himself applies to the child, the name *Emmanuel*. These three items form the core of the Christmas event.

Theologian William Barclay tells us that, in the theology of the Jewish people, the Holy Spirit of God had certain definite functions. Chief among these was the Spirit's role in bringing God's truth to the people. It was the Spirit of God that inspired the prophets of old. "It was the Holy Spirit who taught the prophets what to say" (*Daily Study Bible: Matthew*, Nashville, TN: Westminster John Knox Press, 2001). Now, in today's Gospel, the Holy Spirit's role is not to speak another word of God through another prophet but, marvelously, to allow the entire word of God to be conceived and born of the Virgin Mary. Just as the earth was created through the Word of God, now it will be re-created through the Word made man.

The name that the angel tells Joseph to give the child is *Jesus*. What does *Jesus* mean? It is a form of the name *Joshua*. It means "he shall save [his people] from sin." Names often signified vocations or the special work a person was called upon to do. Jesus' calling is to save from sin—to be the Savior. It is sin that puts distance between us and God. The child of Christmas will save us from our sins and from the distance they put between ourselves and God.

Once the distance is removed God is able to come close to us, even to be with us. And so, Matthew gives the child to be born a name associated in the Old Testament with the majestic God enthroned. It is the name *Emmanuel,* and it means "God-with-us." In his book *New Testament Message: Matthew* (Collegeville, MN: Liturgical Press, 1990), scripture scholar John P. Meier writes: "It is precisely by removing sin from his people that Jesus removes the accursed distance and makes God present among his people."

For you and I to celebrate a Christmas that means more than just its tinsel and its trappings, we need to appreciate these insights that Matthew offers of the child of Christmas. Through Mary's child, the Holy Spirit will restore and renew the face of the earth. Because of Mary's child, God's people will be saved from their sins, and the distance between them and their God, removed. In Mary's child, God will be born in time, among us, and in our personal life stories. "In the beginning was the Word, the Word was with God, and the Word was God. . . . And the Word became flesh and made his dwelling among us" (John 1:1, 14). These are the reasons why Christmas is truly joy to the world and joy in our hearts.

# 14ABC The Nativity of the Lord

## December 25 / Mass at Midnight

## LUKE 2:1–14

### Our Winter's Light

I wish you, dear regular parishioners, a merry and blessed Christmas. I wish you, our visitors here for Christmas, a merry and blessed Christmas. I wish you among us tonight who may be distanced from the Church for whatever reason, a merry and blessed Christmas. We are all God's family, and he is delighted that all of us are worshipping here together on this blessed night of his Son's birth. All of us belong at the manger—no exceptions.

Much of the story of Christmas is a story of light in darkness. Christ is born in the night. He is born in the dark of winter. But a bright light appears in the dark sky. And the angels light up the night sky with the glory of God that surrounds them as they sing their hosannas. And most important of all, the world that has been chained in the long night of sin and error receives its awaited liberation of light. The prophet Isaiah promised it 700 years in advance: "The people who walked in darkness / have seen a great light; / Upon those who dwelt in the land of gloom / a light has shone" (Isaiah 9:1). The infant in the manger is that promised light.

When I wish you a merry Christmas, what does that mean? The Russian novelist Fyodor Dostoyevsky wrote: "While we are on earth, we grope . . . as though in the dark. . . . But for the precious image of Christ before us, we would lose our way." (*Memoirs from the House of the Dead* (New York: Oxford University Press, 2001). Cardinal Newman wrote, "Lead, kindly light, amid the encircling gloom, lead Thou me on; the night is dark, and I am far from home, lead Thou me on" (*Lead Kindly Light: A Devotional Sampler*, Orleans, MA: Paraclete Press). Dylan Thomas wrote, "Light breaks where no sun shines"

("Light Breaks where No Sun Shines" from *The Poetry of Dylan Thomas, New Revised Edition*, New York: New Directions, 2003).

Many of us today are a bit lost in a sort of dark, experiencing a sort of encircling gloom. We are not always able to name it. It's a feeling, a sense we have, dissatisfaction within. It may be the gloom of disillusioned love, the dark of sin, the night of addiction, the dark of depression, the winter of pain and loss, the gloom of short-term contracts and repossessed autos, the dark of inquiries and audits. Many of us are working our heads off in the economy and still wonder what it's all about. We get some release through our wild weekends, our trips to Vegas or New York, and the NFL on wide-screen, high definition TV. But after a year, or two, or three of this we feel like, "Is that all there is to life?"—a sort of gloom, a sort of fog, a sort of dark, a sort of night?

Christmas says, "That's not all there is to it!" Christmas says, "You need something more and there is something more!" Christmas says, "The people who walk in darkness have seen a great light!" Dylan Thomas says, "Light breaks where no sun shines!" Newman says, "Lead, kindly light!" Dostoyevsky says, "We grope as though in the dark. . . . But for the precious image of Christ before us, we would lose our way."

This night, Christ is born among us and for us. Accept him into your heart. Walk through life with him at your side. He will put light and meaning on everything that crosses your path. And he will love and cherish you every step of the way. To wish you a merry Christmas is to wish that Christ be born not just in Bethlehem of Judea but in the Bethlehem of your heart; not just in the winter straw of a poor manger far away, but in the warm love of your responding heart. And I do wish you that merry Christmas!

# 15ABC The Nativity of the Lord

**December 25 / Mass at Dawn**

## LUKE 2:15–20

### The Poverty of Christmas

Christmas Present—to use an expression from Charles Dickens's *A Christmas Carol*—is a time of plenty. Our hearts fill with joy. The logs on our fires are heaped high. Our tables overflow. Our greetings and gifts to each other are many, and lovingly so. All of this is as it should be because Christmas Present is a time of festival and celebration, and all of us who follow the Lord know the reason why: "And the Word became flesh and made his dwelling among us, and we saw his glory, the glory of the Father's only Son, full of grace and truth" (John 1:14). "From his fullness," writes Saint John, "we have all received, grace in place of grace" (John 1:15) or, as the New American Bible (NAB) footnote more pointedly allows, "grace upon grace."

By way of contrast to the plenty of Christmas Present is the poverty of Christmas Past. By Christmas Past I mean the first Christmas long ago. I think that the most touching thing about Christmas Past is the sheer poverty of the event. It takes place in Bethlehem. The little town of Bethlehem was a poor place at the time of Christ's birth. It was little more than a caravan stop for traders on the edge of the Judean wilderness. On that first Christmas, the little town would have been hosting these traders and, no doubt, the robbers who intended to waylay them at a future time. Bethlehem was likely hosting some others too: the people with some financial clout who had come to register in the great census of Caesar Augustus. Are these the reasons why there was no room for Mary and Joseph in the inn?

In the story of the birth of Christ, the physical setting is poor and all of its actors are poor. Its circumstances are the circumstances of poverty. Jesus was not born in a palace but in a stable. His mother was not surrounded by servants but by a few animals lending her the warmth of their breath. The baby did not lie in laced linen but in sparse straw. His arrival was not celebrated by the powerful of the land but by poor shepherds tending their flock. And who were these shepherds? They were "the untouchables" of Israel. They were listed among "the unclean" or "the people of the land" or "the country people" (as different translations of the New Testament describe them) by the Pharisees who frowned on them. They were the ritually unclean. They lived as permanent nomads in the valleys and on the hills with their flocks. In winter, they had only the shelter of heaped-up stones or caves in the sides of the hills. They lived in the unhygienic circumstances of their calling. They were not able to observe the prescribed ritual washings and were, therefore, unclean in the eyes of the religious establishment.

For all their poverty and filth and lack of breeding, theologian and scripture scholar William Barclay says this of the shepherds in his book *The Gospel of Luke: Daily Study Bible Series* (Nashville, TN: Westminster John Knox Press, 2001): "It is most likely that these Christmas shepherds were in charge of the flocks from which the Temple offerings were chosen. It is a lovely thought that the shepherds who looked after the Temple lambs were the first to see the Lamb of God who takes away the sin of the world."

It is an even lovelier thought, I feel, that the Son of God chose to be born in poverty, of poor parents, among poor shepherds, at the famished time of the year, and that in this humbling way he did what the beloved disciple John said he wanted to do: "he came to . . . his own" (John 1:11). But his own, of course, did not accept him. "His own" were God's chosen people, and "his own" was even the inhospitable holy land itself on which the chosen people lived in expectation of their messiah.

Here is one of the great tragedies of history—that the Messiah's own did not recognize him, that his own did not accept him. But their loss turned out to be our gain. And we are immensely blessed in our gain. For as John says: "But to those who did accept him he gave power to become children of God" (John 1:12). You and I have accepted him. We are the Gentiles who have become the children of God, and the children of his Church, and the children of his kingdom. May you and I, then, on this great day give glory to God from joyous hearts. And may we look back from our abundant Christmas Present to that impoverished Christmas Past and be full of love and gratitude for those whose poverty made possible our plenty.

# 16ABC The Nativity of the Lord

**December 25 / Mass during the Day**

## JOHN 1:1–18

### The Mystery of God's Love

I wish you, dear people, a blessed Christmas. May it mean the birth of Jesus in the stable of your heart with all his healing and comfort and love for you and for those you hold dear.

Some of us here this morning are not regular churchgoers; some of us are. Even among the regulars there are, most likely, many shades of faith. This may be because our faith has been bruised a bit by a failed marriage, or by our children's fall from faith despite our prayers, or by the scandal of religious hate and terrorism, or by the growing secularization of society which whittles away at our spiritual core. Those of us who are not regular churchgoers may be so for no greater reason than that we've lost the habit of it somewhere along the road of life. In all of our cases, the heart has its reasons for whatever deep or shallow faith we swim in, and I am no one's judge. Rather, I'd like to be your support in some small way.

All of us came here to church this morning despite our varying degrees of faith. This means that Christmas is still important to us, whatever our motives are for being here. We may wonder if we're really here just to please the spouse, or the kids, or to keep tongues from wagging, or because of custom, sentiment, nostalgia, and the ghost of a dearly loved grandma. Perhaps it doesn't matter all that much. Perhaps any one of these less-than-perfect motives is, nonetheless, the grace that God uses to draw us here in worship so that he may touch us once more with his love.

You may have read items telling you that Christmas is just the Christian makeover of an old pagan feast—such as the birth of the sun in ancient Egypt which was said to occur on our Christmas night. You may wonder if it's just the echo of an earlier human form of winter celebration. You may wonder if Christmas is largely based on the gathering long ago of the family, the tribe, around a roaring fire to affirm life at the lowest time of the year and to shake a collective fist in the face of the frosty god of winter.

John, in today's Gospel, says that Christmas is much more. He says it's the celebration of the mystery of God's love for you and for me. Christmas means that God's love took human form in the baby born in the stable in Bethlehem. In this way, God made his invisible love for us visible, his intangible heart tangible.

In today's Gospel, John speaks of Christmas with the hindsight of the years he spent in the company of the Christmas child that grew up and became Jesus of Nazareth. It is John's experience of Jesus of Nazareth that allows him to tell us that the Christmas infant is more than a helpless babe in the straw. The infant is the beginning human form of the Word of God, full of grace and truth. The life and the ministry of the adult Jesus proved it for John. Jesus turned out to be the forgiveness of God for poor sinners and God's warmth and love and light in the darkness of our winter world.

Jesus turned out to be the power by which John (and you and I) is able to answer the age-old questions that trouble our friends and contemporaries and maybe even ourselves at times: What's it all about? Why am I here? What might give deeper meaning and purpose to my life? Who can guarantee me a future beyond the grave that seems to end everything?

John found his answers in the baby of Bethlehem who became Jesus of Nazareth. We and our questioning friends can too. In Jesus we are able to live lives of purpose and fulfillment and inner joy. Jesus is the pattern and the power of what each one of us is called to be and can be: a graced human being, a child of God, a person with purpose, someone with a future.

We *are* worthwhile. Christmas means that we are *very* worthwhile in God's eyes. For all our bruises and our failures and our sins, and whether we are regulars or irregulars in our faith and at Sunday worship, we are called by God and we are the beloved of God. You and I, dear friends, are worth the Christmas that God's love makes possible for us. That is what the infant in the manger is telling each one of us this blessed Christmas Day.

# 17ʙ The Holy Family of Jesus, Mary, and Joseph

## Sunday within the Octave of Christmas

### Luke 2:22–40 (longer) or Luke 2:22, 39–40 (shorter)

### A Family Affair

I think it is clear to all of us that having a family and taking care of it is the most challenging job on the planet. I salute all parents, and I thank my own whom the Lord has long since taken to their reward.

Because of the time invested in children and the financial cost of raising and educating them, parenting has to be one long aggravation or one long labor of love. I suppose it's a combination of both. I can understand the quip of the novelist and social critic Gore Vidal who wrote, "Never have children, only grandchildren" (*Two Sisters*, New York: Heinemann, 1970).

The scene described in today's Gospel is called, rather too simply, the presentation of Jesus in the temple. He is brought to the temple because his parents have a lot more to do for him there than just present him to God as a firstborn male. They have a raft of legal requirements to fulfill on behalf of their child. But that is another story. Today, we'll just look at Simeon's prophecy concerning the child, and its implications for his mother.

Simeon says that the child is set to be a sign of contradiction. I don't imagine that any parent would feel at ease if someone were to say such a thing in prophecy about their child. Nor would any parent wish to hear that their child will be the instrument by which their nation will be divided, with some people lifted up and others cast down because of him. Simeon is prophesying that Jesus will be what we call "a watershed event" in the history of his people. A glance at that history shows that the child eventually did divide his nation into those who accepted him as Messiah and those who rejected him. He divided his people bitterly, but he did it in the cause of God's truth and their salvation.

You and I must accept the hard fact that Jesus continues to divide people. "I have come," he later said, "to bring not peace but the sword" (Matthew 10:34). If you follow the Lord in the pro-life movement, for example, you may find enemies even on the street where you live. If you champion the sacrament of Marriage as a Christian non-negotiable, you may find yourself at odds with your own family if you have a relative who is in a non-sacramental partnership. If you are scrupulous about your taxes you may find others in the parish who are not, and who do not look on you as particularly moral but as particularly extreme. Fudging is in the compromised religion many of us follow, and fiddling is in the social air we all breathe.

Simeon prophesied that the child would reveal our inner hearts. Normally, we try to hide our inner hearts. Shakespeare said that all of us are actors. We are actors on the stage of life. "All the world's a stage, / and all the men and women merely players" (*As You Like It*, Act II). Actors used to wear masks to give them the different faces that matched the different characters and emotions they were playing. According to the psychologists, all of us wear masks as we try to hide our inner hearts. We wear different faces in public and we hide behind our masks to cloak our anxiety and our sin. These faces and masks actually reveal something—what the Bible calls the deviousness of the human heart (see Jeremiah 17:9).

"My heart is a lonely hunter that hunts on a lonely hill," writes Fiona Macleod ("The Lonely Hunter"). We hunt hidden in our camouflages. I think that each of us remains a lonely and compromising hunter on the lonely hill of life until we meet Jesus. Then, it's unmasking time! If we take him seriously, we find that he insists that we drop all the pretences and that, to the contrary, we start defining ourselves solely through his transparent word, but with his enabling grace. Jesus forces me to reveal who I really am, and where I stand in relation to him.

"And you yourself a sword will pierce," Simeon said to Mary. He was foretelling her immense grief during the suffering and death of her son. Naturally, being a man, I have little appreciation of the personal side of a mother's anguish. Only a mother who loses her sweet child has. And in later years, only a mother can live the anguish of naming all the hours and all the hopes and all the secrets that once passed in small words between herself and her child. And I have only a poor sense of the public side of a mother's anguish, the piercing of the sword of sorrow through her heart when she heard the blood-thirsty curses and watched the public execution of her golden child.

In Blessed Anne Catherine Emmerich's private vision of Calvary (*The Dolorous Passion of Our Lord Jesus Christ*, Rockford, IL: TAN Books, 1994), it is the soldier's lance that turns out to be the sword of Simeon's prophecy: "Mary looked as if the lance had transfixed her heart instead of that of her divine Son, and could scarcely support herself." Since you and I are part of God's family, we must expect the sword of anguish to pierce our hearts too. Our solidarity with Jesus and his mother requires it. We don't have to seek out our share of the sword. It all too easily finds us. Standing for Christ's vision of life and for his standards, in these days of contention and counter-values, will bring the sword into our hearts. We must not be surprised if it is wielded not just by familiar enemies but by loved ones and friends as well.

# 18ABC The Blessed Virgin Mary, Mother of God

**January 1 / The Octave Day of Christmas**

## LUKE 2:16–21

### Following the Yellow Brick Road

My first order of pastoral business today is to wish you a happy new year. And, indeed, I do. May it be a happy and a graceful year for all of us.

It's that time again when we do our Dorothy from Kansas thing and "follow the yellow brick road" to the wonderful land of Oz. I suppose that our version of Oz is, these days, the land of healthful and holistic living, and the yellow brick road is the road that's paved with our new year's resolutions in that regard.

The usual resolutions are again staking their claims with us. There's that midriff bulge that calls for a diet. There's that shortness of breath calling for regular exercise. There's that short fuse that gave everyone in the family their Christmas-on-the-edge. There's that near-accident on the day after Christmas that just might be attributable to drink even though you remember having only one or two. And there's still the same old crowd at the office waiting to suffer through another year from your shadow side.

What to do? What to do? The Gospel tells us that, about this time of year, Mary was reflecting upon certain things in her heart. She was reflecting upon the things she had heard the shepherds say about her child. She was treasuring above all the remarkable words of the angels to the shepherds, "Today in the city of David a savior has been born for you who is Messiah and Lord" (Luke 2:11).

The first thing I want to say to you, dear friends, is that this single statement is the original Christian Gospel properly so called. It is the original "Good News" (Luke 2:10) from God. Jesus is the Messiah; Jesus is the Lord; Jesus is the Savior. It is above all else, these staggering definitions of her child as Messiah, Lord, and Savior that Mary reflects upon and—as most translations have it—treasures in her heart.

This original "gospel of the angels" later becomes the Church's Gospel and the basic confession of Christian faith. It is Jesus alone, writes Saint Paul, that God has put forward "as [our] expiation, through faith, by his blood" (Romans 3:25). Jesus, Mary's child, is our sole Savior and the world's sole Savior. Saint Peter says, "There is no salvation through anyone else, nor is there any other name under heaven given to the human race by which we are to be saved" (Acts 4:12). It is because of his saving service in our regard that God exalts Jesus as the glorious Lord. Saint Peter then says, "Therefore let the whole house of Israel know for certain that God has made him both Lord and Messiah, this Jesus whom you crucified" (Acts 2:36). This original and fundamental Gospel is, effectively, missing in much of the Western world. It has little real meaning even in some Christian lives today.

Why is this tragically so? There are many possible reasons. Maybe it's because some of us feel we have no worthwhile sins and therefore we feel no great need of a Savior. We define real sin by using the backdrop of TV's daily doses of bombs and bullets and terrorists and serial killers and big-time fraud. Against this backdrop, we find little "real" sin coursing through our veins or troubling the small private world we inhabit. Or maybe it's because the claims of so many religions and deities these days, and the ecumenical respect we are expected to show all of them, lessen our sense of the uniqueness of Jesus as the sole Savior and Jesus as Lord.

Or perhaps our present-day social and personal agendas (involving our legitimate concerns over jobs, transportation, housing, careers, personal health, etc.) push the traditional religious agenda to the side and require a set of social saviors different from the religious one we relied upon in less stressful and more faithful times. There are many reasons why the original Christian Gospel of Jesus as the sole Savior and Lord is effectively missing in some lives.

One new year resolution we might consider is this image we have in today's Gospel of Mary treasuring in her heart what the angels said to the shepherds about her son. He is the long-awaited Savior. He is God's anointed one. He is the Lord of life and of glory.

By God's decree, all of human history and all our personal histories must pass through him. Otherwise they pass into nothingness.

We could resolve, in this new year, to spend a few minutes each day reflecting on the scriptures at home or re-reading at home the Sunday that we heard proclaimed at the liturgy earlier in the day. I think I can guarantee you that in the quiet time you spend treasuring the Lord's word, with the Spirit at your shoulder, you will come to know your Savior and your Lord with a freshness and a feeling—and a relevance to the social agenda and to your personal agenda—that you haven't experienced since you first encountered him when you were a marveling child.

Let a deeper encounter with the Lord, with the Lord of your life and of the stages of your personal history, be your resolution for this new year. Let the path of the Gospels be the yellow brick road you choose to take this year to the land of better Christian living. St. Thérèse of Lisieux wrote in her *Story of a Soul: The Autobiography of St. Therese of Lisieux* (ICS Publications, 1991), "Above all, it's the gospels that occupy my mind. I'm always finding fresh light there." You will too, concerning yourself and your life, and your relationship with your sole Savior and Lord.

# 19ABC Second Sunday after Christmas

## JOHN 1:1–18 (LONGER) OR JOHN 1:1–5, 9–14 (SHORTER)

### Crib and Cosmos

Since Christmas, the readings of the liturgy have been giving us as full a picture as they can of Jesus. The liturgy has been at pains, as it were, to draw out for us the range of meaning that may be found in the child that was born on Christmas Day.

Thus, we've had readings about the infant in the manger who is a helpless baby in the straw. We learn from this that God makes himself vulnerable and trusts himself to our care. The angel tells us that the infant is also, in fact, the long-awaited Savior of God's people, and we are challenged to resurrect our sense of sin. Then we meet this infant later as the remarkable child in the temple, discussing the Law with the learned rabbis, and giving us the hint of his future as the teacher of Israel and the light of all nations. Today, through the soaring theological mind of John, we meet the infant as the cosmic Christ. For he, too, was born on that first Christmas Day.

John writes for people of a Hellenistic (i.e., Greek) background. They are people with a philosophical frame of mind. John does not wish to present Jesus to them through a Jewish theology. They would be lost in its Jewish categories. He goes straight to the philosophy they understand. They are a people who admire the *logos* (the word or the mind of God) that create the orderliness and the beauty of the world. And so, he pens this wonderful prologue: "In the beginning was the *logos*-Word . . . The *logos*-Word was with God . . . All things were created through the *logos*-Word . . . And in the fullness of time that *logos*-Word became flesh and lived among us." Now, let me tell you his whole story! Let me uncover for you this Word and Wisdom that you so admire! It is actually a person. It is the Son of God. His name is Jesus of Nazareth.

Our generation is characterized by its concern for the human and the personal. What does being human mean? What does person-hood entail? How does one achieve true humanity and full personhood? The whole world has an opinion on these questions and, perhaps, we are confused by the plethora of opinions.

TV and radio talk shows offer definitions of the human and the personal. So do celebrities. So does every homespun guru. Psychology and philosophy offer critically thought-out descriptions. So does Pope John Paul II. He never stops. Apart altogether from his position as Pope, he is a considerable philosopher on this issue of human-ness and personhood. No wonder young people flocked to him. They are looking for their self-identity. He's always at work defining for them who they are. According to John Paul II, one becomes truly human by living the pattern that God set in the humanity of Jesus, and one reaches the highest level of personhood when one's human potential reaches its full maturity through grace. That can only happen in Christ. Saint Paul says the same thing. So does Saint John.

Was it Macbeth who said that life is "but a walking shadow"? Was it Sartre who said that a human being is just "a useless passion"? Was it Yeats who wished to "unriddle the universe"? Today's Gospel says that the Word of God, the cosmic Christ, is the one who unriddles the universe and the one who defines the human person as no science or technology ever will. So what are we doing? Are we putting Christ forward to our anxious world as its pattern of personhood? Are we telling our confused youth and our semi-agnostic fellow workers that life can be just as questionable for us as it is for them but that, in Christ, we have a handle on the mystery? Are we telling suicidal young students that Jesus is the key to treasures of comfort and support greater than all exam anxieties and all growing-up stresses, and deeper than all the TV commercials that claim to offer them great taste, gusto, and even life? Dear young parishioners: Don't live life to the power of a commercial! Live life to the power of Christ!

So many others—gunmen, thugs, street gang members, addicts—are loose on our mean modern streets because they are adrift of Christ and have lost the sense of what is human and precious in their victims and in themselves. All that can be changed in Christ! Are we ourselves content to stay with our childish version of Christianity, the version that fails us—and fails the teens we model for—in the ambushes of life? Do we not wish to grow into adult faith, and experience the depth of God's love now in this life that John and the others came to know in such a fulfilling way?

Trite theology and panic prayers are not worthy of Christ and of the Christian faith in an educated and questioning age. All of us need to prioritize Jesus the Word in our everyday agenda, and we need a seriously reflective engagement with the Gospels about that Word so that we may know what it is to be human and how one achieves optimum personhood. Only then will we have an adult grip on this "Word [that] became flesh and made his dwelling among us" (John 1:14). Only then will we have a fitting adult experience that parallels John's. We ought to be able to say what he was able to say of himself and of the other disciples: "From Christ's fullness we have all received, grace upon grace" (John 1:16).

# 20ABC The Epiphany of the Lord

## MATTHEW 2:1–12

### The Meaning of the Magi

*Epiphany* means the showing forth. The baby born in Bethlehem is shown forth, or presented, in this lovely story of the magi (or wise men or kings or astrologers), as the Savior of all the nations and not only of his own people, Israel. Just as there is equal rights and equal opportunity these days, so is there equal opportunity of salvation for all of God's children in the Savior born in Bethlehem.

The main point of the story, then, is to have the magi, as the representatives of all the nations, present at the birth of the world's Savior. In them, our Gentile forebears, you and I—of all races and of all colors—were present when Christ was born. Before that moment, we were religious outsiders to God and to grace. But through the magi we were chosen for intimacy with the Lord.

The gifts that the magi placed at the foot of the manger were gold, frankincense, and myrrh. Gold symbolized kingship, incense symbolized divinity. Early Christian tradition understood these gifts as signaling the kingship and the divinity of Jesus. Myrrh was seen as a prophecy about the child's future death, since myrrh was a resin that was used in perfume and in the anointing of the body for burial. We may interpret the magi's gifts in that manner.

Another interpretation is possible. Magi appear elsewhere in the New Testament scriptures as magicians, or practitioners of the black arts. Examples are Simon Magus and Elymas the magician. In this interpretation, the magi were magicians—outsiders to the world of orthodox religion—who gave up the instruments of their shady trade when they met the Infant. Incense/smoke hid the magician's subterfuge, and myrrh/resin/adhesive gum made objects marvelously disappear (stuck to your arm under your sleeve!). Gold stands for the ill-gotten profit of their art. They surrendered it all as their darkness gave way to the light of Christ. All falsehood and all false values should surrender to the light of Christ.

Either interpretation is rich in meaning for us. It's time for us to make our own journey of faith to the Infant, following his star and not our own. It's time to surrender the darkness of our false values to the light of his true values. It's time to place at his feet the instruments of our black arts that are the works of darkness we do against conscience, God, and neighbor.

It's time for us to offer the Savior our most prized gold, which is our heart; the incense that is genuine prayer from the heart; and the myrrh that is our works of love for others. It's time for us older Christians especially—after so many Christmases—to be wise men and women who walk with commitment in the light of Christ and whose hearts are always pining for their place at the manger of their salvation.

# 21B The Baptism of the Lord

**Sunday after January 6**
**First Sunday in Ordinary Time**

## MARK 1:7–11

### A Statement about Service

Jesus did not need a baptism of repentance, for he was the sinless one. This is indicated by the surprise of John the Baptist when Jesus presented himself for baptism.

How are we to understand his baptism then? The biblical scholars have a number of suggestions. Some suggest that Jesus underwent John's baptism as an act of solidarity with his fellow Jews who were flocking to John. John the Baptist had stirred them to repentance, and Jesus wished to encourage that repentance in them. Others suggest that Jesus was capitalizing on the new religious fervor, that he was taking advantage of this groundswell of fervor in order to shape it to his own mission as the Messiah. Theologian William Barclay puts this more graciously by quoting Shakespeare, "There is a tide in the affairs of men, which, taken at the flood, leads on to fortune" (*Julius Caesar*, IV, Scene 3).

At any rate, Jesus' baptism was not baptism as we understand it. His baptism had nothing to do with personal sin and personal repentance.

If we look at the First Reading of today's liturgy, I think we find a more engaging suggestion as to why Jesus underwent baptism. The reading contains the opening lines of Isaiah, chapter 42. These opening lines make up the first of the so-called Songs of the Messianic Servant. Jesus is the Servant of God, the "Man for others" in Dietrich Bonhoeffer's phrase, and his baptism may well be a ritual cleansing to mark the start of his Servant ministry. If it is, then his baptism is his statement in public of the ministry he is now embarking upon with full acceptance and lasting commitment.

The Lord's baptism is a statement about service. So, in part, should be every Christian's Baptism. Emerging from the water, Jesus' commitment is sealed by the Spirit; and he and his mission are approved by the Father's voice in the hearing of all of Israel.

Every African missionary has heard of the legendary Nobel laureate Albert Schweitzer. He is the genius who, a few generations ago, left his place at the pinnacle of European scholarship to build his leper hospital on the bank of a river in Africa. There he practiced his singular Christian insight: reverence for life on all levels and in all its forms.

Schweitzer wished on us the blessing of finding the secret of a happy life. He said it is service to others. He hoped we would make the discovery early in our lives, lest we make it only at the door of death, with wistful regret.

Jesus is the servant of God and the servant of others. We are too, in solidarity with him.

The elements of Christian service are found in the Servant songs of Isaiah, in the commandments and beatitudes of Jesus, and, of course, in the life and ministry of Jesus. Long ago, the Church made it easy for us to know these elements of Christian service by composing for us its list of "the spiritual and corporal works of mercy." We are strong on the corporal works today, such as feeding the hungry, clothing the naked, and visiting our less fortunate brothers and sisters who are ill and in prison. Even the so-called secular world is greatly involved in these corporal works of mercy. And that is as it should be, thank God.

But we are not too strong on the spiritual works, especially knowledge of the faith. This is the great weakness in the ministry of the Church over the past generation and today. Too many people know far too little about the faith these days. Therefore, you and I should challenge ourselves with regard to these spiritual works. Are we instructing the ignorance of the faith that is widespread in our time? Especially adult faith? Are we counseling and encouraging and challenging, as needs be, those among family members and friends and parishioners with doubts of faith and experiences of addiction and moral difficulty of various kinds? Are we pulling our weight for Christ and for his kingdom in the modern marketplace of ideas and lifestyles where others, with so much less to offer, are confidently active? It's our call.

There is no reason why we should fail to see our own Baptism in Christ, like his in the Jordan, as our statement of service to others for the sake of the kingdom of God.

# Lent

# 23B First Sunday of Lent

## MARK 1:12–15

### Weary of the World's Empires

Our Lord fasts and prays for 40 days in preparation for his mission of establishing the kingdom of God on earth. Satan tries everything he can to divert our Lord from his mission. You and I are about to go through our Lent of 40 days as an act of solidarity with Jesus, and as our own attempt to establish more securely the kingdom of God in our hearts.

What is the kingdom of God? Basically, it is God's loving sway over our hearts and God's rules for living in the conduct of our daily lives. At a wider sweep, it is our building, in partnership with God, of a better, more just and more loving society here in our country and all around the world.

Social history is the story of humankind's attempts to build a better world. It is a story of success and failure, a story of the good and the bad and the indifferent social systems that we have tried over the course of the centuries. The world has only recently emerged from generations of one kind of social system—imperialism. All of us, I trust, are glad to be out from under it. As far back as 1899, William Butler Yeats may have sensed the coming close of empire in his poem, "The Valley of the Black Pig." There he speaks of his generation as a generation weary of empire and dreaming of a new social dawn.

Unfortunately, the world is not yet finished with empires. Imperialism still lives, but in new forms. Have some countries exchanged the old set of political empires for a new set of economic ones? Are the vast multi-national corporations actually empires in their own right? Are we in the Western nations just an auxiliary of a new empire? I only ask the question so that we may become more conscious of where the products we buy come from, and under what human cost conditions they are produced. There are people by the tens of millions around the world who are reduced in their humanity and marginalized in their poverty, as so many colonial generations were, by the new empires of economic exploitation. We must not just shop until we drop, but stop and think before we shop.

Then there's that other imperialism that's still in our bones, the imperial tendencies of the individual heart. Francis Thompson said that "all man's Babylons strive but to impart the grandeurs of his Babylonian heart" ("The Heart: Two Sonnets"). The Babylon of history was, on one hand, a construct of legal and architectural grandeur under Hammurabi and its other kings but, on the other hand, it was infamous as the Babylon of the Jewish captivity and the tears of the exiles. All too often, man's Babylonian heart expresses his arrogance in the face of God and his imperialism in the face of the poor of the earth.

The imperialism of the heart takes many forms. It is the imperialism of egotism and greed, the imperialism that uses and abuses people no matter what new or wonderful social system they live under. It is the imperialism that treats the home as one's personal fiefdom and one's spouse and children as one's property and possessions. It is the imperialism that makes everyone in the office and at work feel inferior to one's puffed-up self-importance. It is the imperialism of the judgmental mindset that assassinates people's characters in gossip sessions; that financially bleeds the undocumented on the job; that offers indifferent service to the public; and that drives with disregard for life and limb.

Above all, it is the imperialism of the great "I"; me as the center of the universe, my perpetual greediness, and my unrelenting heart. This kind of imperialism is alive and well, at home and abroad, wherever the un-Christlike heart is found. Yet Jesus said to his followers, "I am among you as the one who serves" (Luke 22:26–27).

Jesus, the servant, has assigned a kingdom of service to us. This Lent, we are challenged to test our tight hearts and our taut values against the kingdom of God and its expansive values. We are challenged to be weary of the world's empires and of the imperial tendencies of the human heart.

We are challenged to serve and not to be served. We are challenged to let the curtain drop on a day and on an arrogance that serves no one and, on the contrary, to let new dreams gather around the dawning day of the kingdom of God in our hearts and in our societies.

There is no greater dream on this side of eternity than that of God's kingdom of love and peace and justice in full flood in our hearts and on the earth.

# 26b Second Sunday of Lent

## MARK 9:2–10

### Transfigured in Glory

The incident in today's Gospel is the Transfiguration of Jesus on the mountain. The Transfiguration means that the apostles saw Jesus in a way they had not seen him before. They saw a side of him that was hidden until now. They saw the glory that is his as the eternal Son of God.

W. B. Yeats wrote a poem about another transfiguration which may help us to appreciate this one. It is called "Easter 1916." In 1916, many of the Irish people were involved in their own revolutionary war, similar to the war of independence from Great Britain. Like this war of independence, many of the Irish soldiers were farmers, accountants, factory workers, fathers, brothers, and sons who were asked to do an extraordinary thing in an extraordinary time. In the poem, Yeats speaks of the leaders of the Easter 1916 Irish Rebellion as seemingly ordinary men who were, in fact, quite extraordinary. He thought he knew them as commonplace Dubliners, but Easter 1916 taught him that all the while he knew only one side of them, and that was their least significant side. Hidden beneath their commonplace exterior was the life force of revolution and the vision of a whole new social order. Eventually, their rebellion changed the Irish political and social landscape "utterly."

In the Gospel, Jesus is about to go to Jerusalem and to his death. He goes up the mountain to pray to his Father before this critical event in his life. Perhaps he wants to ask his Father to strengthen him for the journey to Calvary. When the Transfiguration is over, the Lord is steeled in heart and spirit to sacrifice his life for us.

His apostles also need to know something. They need some deeper insight into who their Jesus is. They need to know that he is much more than the persuasive rabbi and the great miracle worker they are familiar with. And they need to be assured that the scandal they will soon find in the cross is not the end; that it is necessary; and that all will end in glory for their Lord and for themselves. He and they are part of a great beauty being born—the salvation of the world, and glory will follow the scandal of the cross.

And so, the Lord is transfigured in glory on the mountain. His face dazzles as the sun and his clothes become as radiant as light. Moses' face once shone on Mount Sinai with the reflected glory of God (see Exodus 34:29). The apostles see a new Jesus on the mountain. It is a preview, as it were, of his future glory beyond the cross.

Moses and Elijah are present. They represent the Law and the prophets. They are in conversation with Jesus. What are they saying? Perhaps they are offering him reassurances as to his cross and, through it, his crown. Peter is so mesmerized by the whole scene that he wants to set up three booths or tents. He recalled, perhaps, how the Israelites once lived in tents in the wilderness, and that they would again live in tents (so it was believed by the Jews) in the messianic age.

A bright cloud overshadows them. It is the *shechinah,* the sunscreen cloud by day and the luminous cloud by night that covered the Israelites during the Exodus, the cloud that signaled the presence of the glory of God. A voice speaks out of the cloud confirming Jesus as God's beloved Son. Our Lord is strengthened and confirmed as to his unique sonship, his necessary cross, and his glorious future beyond it and because of it. The lesson for us can hardly be different. Carrying our daily cross, in imitation of Jesus, is our own prelude to glory.

Transfiguration also means that there is another level to our Christian lives, a dimension that is yet to be. And what a blessed one it is! What happened to Jesus on the mountain will happen to you and to me. One day, being faithful, we too shall be transformed in everlasting glory. We shall be, in the poet Yeats's words, "changed, changed utterly."

# 29B Third Sunday of Lent

## JOHN 2:13–25

### My Father's House

Daniel Defoe wrote (in *The True-Born Englishman*): "Wherever God erects a house of prayer, / The Devil always builds a chapel there." I take these words to mean that we human beings, rather than Satan as such, always find a way of bringing the bad into the good. We do so because there is another house called the house of the human heart, and it is a divided house. Our divided heart tarnishes all things good with a measure of the bad.

And so, whether we are clergy or laity, we bring our divided heart with us wherever we go. We bring our weaknesses and our sinfulness into God's house. That would not be a problem as such if we were merely weak but humble sinners. But we are far more than that. We are prideful and we are pushy. Our pride and our pushiness take wing and do not rest until God's house has a devil's chapel in it. We make God's house a carbon copy of our divided heart.

That's precisely what happened to God's temple in Jerusalem in today's Gospel story. The divided human heart invaded it. David and Solomon had built the temple as the great national sanctuary of God and his people. In the course of the years it had been raided by foreigners, destroyed by the Babylonians, rebuilt by the returning exiles, and was in the process of further development and embellishment under King Herod in our Lord's time. But what did our Lord find when he went up to the temple to pray on the great feast of Passover?

He found his own people turning part of God's temple into a holding pen for animals, into a meat market, and into a money house. People haggled over prices, sometimes swore at each other, and sometimes came to blows—all in God's house! It is easy to appreciate Jesus' righteous anger at the behavior of his fellow-countrymen. He cries out in anguish, "Take these out of here and stop making my Father's house a marketplace!"

Now the temple as a place of sacrifice had to have a certain commercialism attached to it. Animals had to be penned there, sold there, and offered in sacrifice there. The money-changers had to be there to accommodate the Jewish worshippers who came from all parts of the Roman Empire with their foreign coins. Those coins— foreign and ritually unclean—had to be exchanged for Jewish *shekels*. That was the task of the money-changers. In addition, every working Jewish male had to pay the temple tax; so the clatter of coins resounded in the temple courtyards and echoed into the sanctuary and into the Holy of Holies. All of these things were necessary. So why was Jesus incensed?

For one thing, says the biblical scholar William Barclay, animals that were bought outside of the temple precincts were subject to an additional inspection tax. This was done, apparently, to pressure the people into buying within the temple precincts and thus enlarging the financial take of the temple officials. Barclay tells us that the inspected animals were likely to be rejected in favor of the temple animals which cost several times more. He also tells us that the whole costly enterprise practically ruled out the poor from observing their religious duty. In other words, the temple worship had degenerated into exploitation and extortion. And since the Bible favors the poor because the poor always come off second best in this world, it was disgusting to see that they were also coming off second best in the temple and in their ability to worship God. Jesus was incensed at this mistreatment of the poor.

He was also incensed, according to Barclay, because this whole temple scene had become "worship without reverence" (*Daily Study Bible: John,* Nashville, TN: Westminster John Knox Press, 2001). Jesus used the occasion to prophesy that this form of worship and these sacrifices would come to an end. So would the very temple itself. There would be a new temple, an entirely different temple. In the future, the true worship of God would pass through the temple that is Jesus himself and those who are incorporated in him through grace.

In this sense, the new temple is the human heart redeemed and graced by Christ. The new temple is the Christian heart. It is your heart and my heart. Our heart is God's new house. We cannot let it degenerate as the Jerusalem temple degenerated. We cannot allow Satan to have his little chapel in it.

Lent is the time given us each year to spring-clean our temple—with a little fasting, a little more focused prayer, a companioning of Jesus along the stations of his suffering and death, and a renewed heart through the sacrament of reconciliation. All of this may be "old stuff," but surely it is "good stuff." The liturgical directives that came in the wake of the Second Vatican Council may have resulted in the refurbishing of some our churches, but the Council was primarily convened for the renewal of the house of the human heart. It is always the condition of the human heart that matters with our God, and that should matter most with us.

# 32B Fourth Sunday of Lent

## John 3:14–21

### Lifted Up

During the Second World War, on June 22, 1944, three years to the day after Hitler invaded the Soviet Union, the Soviet armies began their great offensive on the Eastern front against the German forces. It did not end until they arrived in Berlin. The Soviet offensive was so huge and so powerful it overwhelmed the decimated German divisions.

In the TV documentary "War of the Century," a German soldier by the name of Heinz Fiedler says, "The word came down the line, 'Flak guns to the front! Anti-tank guns to the front! Ammunition to the front!' The word went back up the line, 'The guns are smashed! There is no more ammunition!' Our troops were getting ever smaller. Then the command came, 'Every man for himself!' We looked to see the position of the sun . . . so we could find the west." It was not easy to spot the position of the sun in the smoke of thousands of Soviet artillery pieces. Another German soldier, Walter Mauth, says, "We young guys were doomed to be in this situation. We just searched for salvation. There is the west! Let's head for the west!" You can imagine the anguish of these youngsters trying to find a way out of the nightmarish situation that Hitler had put them in.

Sometimes, in our own lives, we get ourselves into dire straits and search for salvation. Sometimes nations get themselves into dire straits. So do societies. So do communities. The Bible tells us that the whole human family got itself into a sad state one time with original sin, and that on occasion the effects of that sin still push us, as nations and as individuals, into sad situations. All of us have reason to look for salvation at one time or another in our lives. We look up searching for the position of whatever sun points the way of our release.

Jesus asks us, in today's Gospel, to look up and to see the Son of Man on his cross and, beyond his cross, to see him in the glory of his Resurrection. He wants us to see this "double-lifting up" of himself, as biblical scholar William Barclay puts it, as something he did for us. Whoever believes, he says, in the One lifted up on the cross, and then lifted up in glory, will have eternal life. Nearing the end of his ministry, Jesus repeats that promise: "And when I am lifted up from earth, I will draw everyone to myself" (John 12:32).

We need lifting up from time to time. The contrast, in today's Mass readings, is between lifting up our eyes and looking for salvation or choosing to stay downcast in our sins. It is between allowing ourselves to be lifted up by the grace of Christ or choosing to sit dejectedly by the waters of bitterness, as the Babylonian exiles of the first reading of our liturgy today ended up doing. It is scripture's view that we cause our own sins, and that the sin which we continue to abide eventually brings on spiritual dejection and apathy. It is the same scripture's view that we can be lifted up from our sin, and that salvation is readily available in the Lord raised up in saving grace over us.

Those two German soldiers I mentioned were among the fortunate ones who survived the Soviet cauldron. In their dire straits, they looked up to find the sun that would point them in the direction of the west. Many of their comrades did not, and perished. Some of the Jewish exiles in Babylon eventually looked up in search of the prophets who would lead the return to Jerusalem, and found them. The majority, however, did not and died generation by generation "by the waters of Babylon" (Psalm 137:1).

Jesus was first lifted up on the cross in pain and then lifted up in glory. He said, "When I am lifted up from earth, I will draw everyone to myself" (John 12:32). He didn't speak these words for his benefit, but for ours. They are his promise to us that salvation is there for any one of us who has the need of it and the heart for it.

# 35B Fifth Sunday of Lent

## JOHN 12:20–33

### Dying to Live

Today's Gospel reading is called a gospel of paradoxes. But it is also a gospel of wonderful connections. As Jesus approaches his hour of death, he is also approaching his hour of glory. A grain of wheat must be planted in the earth and die in order for it to live on as next year's harvest. The person for whom this life is everything will lose it very shortly, but the person who loses (i.e., spends) his or her life in the service of others will save it for eternity.

That line, "Whoever loves his life loses it, and whoever hates his life in this world will preserve it for eternal life," rubs some people the wrong way. They think it means that God allows human beings no real freedom in life. They must live their life his way, the holy way, or else! But the "God will get you if you don't do it his way" theology is not the issue here at all. God is not a copy of my petty self, someone "with a bourgeois mind," as the Devil says in C. S. Lewis's *The Screwtape Letters* (San Francisco: HarperSanFrancisco, 2001).

Rather, the Lord is stating two simple facts. One is a fact of nature. The other is a fact of Christianity. First, anyone who tries to hold on to this life by making it as secure as possible must, in the end, lose it anyway. For life on this planet is short, seventy or eighty years in the biblical estimate (see Psalm 90:10). That's a fact of nature. Second, since this life is short, is it is not better for a Christian to spend it serving others, as Jesus spent his life serving others? There is no reward for selfishness beyond the grave. That's a fact of Christianity. And why should there be? Why should anyone's personal greed and self-centeredness be rewarded in the next life as well as in this one?

It is hard to understand Christians who live a self-centered life. It is hard to understand Christians who spend their time in this world expanding their selfishness while contracting their Christianity. That is the opposite of what the trajectory of the Christian life should be. The grain of wheat that does nothing, that just lays there unused in the granary, slowly disintegrates. It accomplishes nothing. Unless it falls into the earth and is buried, it will produce nothing. Christians are the grains of wheat that Jesus has in mind, and he himself is the first of the grains. He was buried in the earth for us and rose up in new life. The early Christians were buried in the persecutions of the Roman Empire and thus they gave birth to the generations of converts who were inspired by their self-sacrifice. Tertullian wrote, "You may crucify us, torture us, condemn us, destroy us. . . . we only increase in number every time you mow us down. The blood of Christians is the seed of the Church" (Apologeticus).

In the same manner, it is only by spending our lives for others that we eventually preserve them for ourselves. Even the so-called secular world remembers nothing of the millions of people who passed this way but contributed little to the well-being of society. But the secular world honors those who spent their lives, or lost their lives, for the sake of cause and country. And God, of course, knows intimately the millions who have spent their lives in his service and on behalf of his children. How could he fail to, since they now surround his throne in heaven? Soon, we will re-live the Passion and death of our Lord in the liturgy of Holy Week.

He is the one who loved us so passionately that he allowed himself to be buried in the earth for our sakes. Is it asking too much that we, in solidarity with him, bury our selfishness and live instead in a manner that brings his love a little more into our families, into our parish, into our relationships, and into the lives of the poor and the displaced in our community? You don't need to ask me what each of these is in need of. You have been around the Gospel and the Church and the parish all of your life.

Your own good judgment and your own best heart already know the answer.

# 37B Palm Sunday of the Lord's Passion

**At the Procession with Palms**

## MARK 11:1–10

### Triumph and Humility

The central Gospel of the liturgy of this day is, of course, the Passion narrative. We will look here at this shorter Gospel of the Lord's triumphal entry into Jerusalem. It is the Gospel that is proclaimed at the blessing of the palms.

It can be read as a Gospel of humility or triumph. Traditionally, we read it as a Gospel of triumph. Even G. K. Chesterton sees it in this light, for he includes the humble donkey, of his famous poem *The Donkey*, in a share of the Lord's triumph.

The massed crowds turn the Lord's entry into Jerusalem into a jubilant occasion. They do not realize, as he does, that he is also entering the city to begin the painful process of his Passion and death. They see this moment as the beginning of a glorious era for themselves, with Jesus as their king. They shout "Hosanna!" It is a word that has deep meaning for them. In Hebrew, it means "Save now!" It is the old Jewish cry from the heart for salvation. No doubt, the salvation that is uppermost in their hearts at this moment is political salvation. Their holy city and their holy nation are polluted with a Gentile presence and a pagan god, with the empire of Rome and its Caesar-God. A fervor has gripped the people's imagination: Jesus is about to restore the kingdom of David! They are thinking of a political restoration.

And so, they declare blessed the one "who comes in the name of the Lord," and they bow their palm fronds in deference before him. The greetings they shout at Jesus are greetings of praise from Psalm 118. In our Bibles, Psalm 118 is titled "A Hymn of Thanksgiving to the Savior of Israel." It celebrates the victory of Judas Maccabeus, several generations previously, over King Antiochus and the deliverance of Israel from foreign domination and religious pollution. The crowds, at this moment, hail Jesus as the new Maccabeus; they sense deliverance from the Romans in him and the restoration of Israel's glory. A few days later they will turn on Jesus because they cannot accept that the kingdom of God must no longer be understood as a kingdom of this world.

But how does a donkey fit in this scene of triumph? Our Lord deliberately chooses the donkey to ride on. He intends this seemingly humiliating choice not as a lesson in humility as such but as a messianic statement about himself. In choosing a donkey to ride on, he is fulfilling the messianic prophecy of the prophet Zechariah: "Rejoice heartily, O daughter Zion, shout for joy, O daughter Jerusalem! See, your king shall come to you; a just savior is he, meek, and riding on a donkey" (Zechariah 9:9).

Furthermore, the donkey was a highly respected animal among the Jewish people. They relied on it for both labor and transportation. The donkey is, as any of us who ever had working experience with one knows, a gentle and a docile creature. Among the Jews, therefore, the donkey was a symbol of peace. Jesus is the Prince of Peace, and the kingdom of God is a kingdom of peace. In riding on the donkey, Jesus is telling the crowds what kind of king he really wants to be, and over what kind of kingdom he wishes to preside.

There is additional symbolism in the donkey as it appears in Jewish scripture. The donkey is a beast of burden. The prophet Isaiah's dominant image of the Messiah to come is the image of a suffering servant. The language Isaiah uses to describe this suffering servant is the language we associate with an animal, with a beast of burden, with a bothered and beaten and overburdened donkey. I suspect that Isaiah, for all the social respect given donkeys, saw some mistreated ones in his time, and I suspect that his theology had no trouble in substituting the burdened and beaten Jesus for one of these mistreated creatures.

If we see today's Gospel story through the lens of Isaiah, we will not be able to separate impending tragedy from this scene of wild triumph. It is Sunday. The donkey carries on its back the one who will carry the burden of our sins to the cross on Friday. There is something deeply engaging about the donkey and Jesus on their fateful journey together today, and in their respective roles. Maybe it's the willingness of the one to carry the weight of our Lord, and the willingness of the other to carry the weight of our sins to the cross.

# Easter Triduum

# 39ABC Holy Thursday

## Evening Mass of the Lord's Supper

## JOHN 13:1–15

### The Gospel of Service

Some years ago, a bank I did business with hit on a new sales pitch: "Service is our most important product." That line ought to stand as a golden rule among Christians. It certainly was a golden rule with Jesus.

On the religious level, our Lord is celebrating Passover with his disciples, and he is about to institute the momentous ritual that we call the Mass. On the personal level, he is about to pass from this world to the Father. At such a critical time, when he should be absorbed in these matters, what does he do? He starts washing feet!

If this were a stage play, the audience would be intrigued by the sudden shift in the plot. It has no apparent relationship with what has been unfolding thus far in the drama of the Passover celebration. It is an about-face, something entirely unexpected. But, obviously, Jesus knew what he was doing—and he intended this change, and this dramatic turn of events, to underline a critical Christian teaching. The teaching is this: service is our most important product. A Christian is born to serve. Our Lord teaches by doing. He picks up the basin. He pours the water into it. He bends down. He does the washing. He does the drying. There is no pious pep talk here, nor stylized ritual. Our Lord's actions are his words. He finishes and asks, "Do you realize (i.e., understand) what I have just done for you? You call me 'teacher' and 'master,' and rightly so, for indeed I am. If I, therefore, the master and teacher, have washed your feet, you ought to wash one another's feet. I have given you a model to follow, so that as I have done for you, you should also do." If we do not understand the centrality of service in the life of the Christian, then we will "have no inheritance" with Jesus.

Our own lives, on the contrary, are full of scrambling for recognition. We are miffed when others do not give us the deference due our titles, or the place of honor our dignity assumes it deserves.

We are all caught up in "the pecking order" syndrome. Everyone wants to be served; many have no great desire to serve. It infects even the Church. Biblical scholar and theologian William Barclay observed: "So often, even in churches, trouble arises because someone does not get his place. So often even ecclesiastical dignitaries are offended because they did not receive the precedence to which their office 'entitled' them. Here (in this Gospel) is the lesson that there is only one kind of greatness, the greatness of service. The world is full of people who are standing on their dignity when they ought to be kneeling at the feet of their brethren" (*Daily Study Bible:* John, Nashville, TN: Westminster John Knox Press, 2000).

I don't want us to hear these words, nod our heads in pious agreement, and go away saying, "What a nice thought!" I want us to believe it in the way Jesus believed it—by doing it as he, our Lord and Master, did as an example for us.

# 40ABC Good Friday of the Lord's Passion

## The Passion of Our Lord Jesus Christ

## MARK 11:1–10

### Were You There?

All great creative literature reflects human life and the human condition. The great novels and stories hinge on characterization, plot, confrontation, conscience, and choice. We find ourselves in the characters of these novels and stories, and in the life situations they find themselves in. We also find ourselves on the pages of that other great corpus of literature, the scriptures.

And so, we find ourselves in one or other of the characters that make up the great drama of Good Friday. When I was a student, the French priest Louis Evely wrote about the Passion and death of

Jesus in that manner, and my reflections here are partly a copy of what I remember from him.

What part do you and I play in this tragedy that is the Passion and death of Jesus? We say, excusing ourselves, that we weren't there, that it all happened two thousand years ago. But Calvary goes on every day. It is repeated every day in some faraway dictatorship and also in our own country; in vast cities like Los Angeles, New York, and Chicago and in the small towns of rural America; in drug-infested inner-city families and in the family we are part of. We may say that we weren't at the original Calvary and, therefore, played no part in the historical suffering and death of Jesus, but we can not say that Calvary does not repeat itself in one form or another in every generation, including our own, and we cannot avoid playing a part in its modern versions.

What part do I play in the drama? Am I Peter, denying my faith in the office or in the warehouse because I lack backbone? Am I Pilate, washing my hands of a decision that demands justice because I'm afraid to upset the higher-ups in my company and in my church? Am I the fickle mob that shouts, "Crucify him! Crucify him!" when a homeless shelter tries to locate on my street? Am I the culturally conditioned soldier who readily mocks and taunts the homeless panhandlers under the cross of his or her agony? Am I the cowardly disciples who flee when the going gets too rough or when people of color come into the neighborhood?

Or, am I the weeping women of Jerusalem who can empathize with a victim because I have a nurturing heart? Am I the Veronica of legend who has the guts to do something and, because of which, I find an impression of Jesus and a grace left on my soul? Am I Simon of Cyrene, no hero and not quite sure what political correctness in the situation calls for, but I let goodness get the better of me? Am I Joseph of Arimathea who risks my social position or my church position because my heart is human? Am I Mary, the mother, who picks up the pieces of a life shattered by the blindness and bigotry of others? When I see today's version of the Victim of Calvary, do my eyes pass over his and her head as though he and she were not there, or do my eyes meet theirs, and answer their pain?

Sometimes I wonder if the reality of Calvary Past and the challenge of Calvary Present are softened, rather than sharpened, in us when we sing the touching lines of "Were You There When They Crucified My Lord?" and when we conduct our devout ritual of Good Friday. I don't wish to undermine the value of either. I only wonder, and I only raise this question in order to underline a critical pastoral point. It is this: It would be a real tragedy for us if we thought that Calvary and its Victim and its cast of characters appeared only once in human history, and that a long, long time ago.

# 41ABC The Vigil in the Holy Night of Easter

## Easter Sunday: The Resurrection of the Lord

## MARK 16:1–7

### Go, and Tell!

In the Easter Gospel that was just proclaimed, the three holy women come to anoint the body of Jesus in the tomb. They are in for some surprises.

First, they find the great stone rolled back from the entrance to the tomb. Then they find the tomb empty. Next, they are amazed at the presence of what appears to them to be a young man. But he is not a man. He is clothed in white, but it is an unusual whiteness. Matthew's version of the same scene reads, "His appearance was like lightning and his clothing white as snow" (Matthew 28:3). He speaks to the women in the apocalyptic manner of a messenger from heaven. His function is to interpret for them the meaning of the empty tomb, which they now see and are perplexed by. He does his job succinctly and well!

One biblical scholar, Wilfrid Harrington, aptly calls him an "interpreting angel" (*Mark: New Testament Message—A Biblical-Theological Commentary*, Collegeville, MN: Michael Glazier, 1979). The interpreting angel tells the three women the joyful news of the Lord's Resurrection. These women are the first to hear it. It is fitting that they should be the first because they were present on Calvary when Jesus died and when he was placed in the tomb. William Barclay calls this favor to the women, "receiving love's reward" (*The Gospel of Matthew: The New Daily Bible Study*, Nashville, TN: Westminster John Knox Press, 2001).

The interpreting angel then says to the women: "Go, and tell his disciples and Peter." The women are to tell the disciples that Jesus is risen and will meet them in Galilee, as he promised them. He will keep his promise despite the fact that they abandoned him at the beginning of his Passion. And Peter is to be told, too. Some may wish to read this singling out of Peter as somehow underpinning his headship of the Church, but such is not the relevant point in my opinion. He is singled out in this instance because of his denial of Jesus in the Garden of Gethsemane. The interpreting angel is not tasked with reminding the disciples and Peter of their sins, only with the Lord's gracious invitation to meet with them in Galilee *despite* their sins. Clearly, our dear Lord overlooks much that was flawed in the disciples' and in Peter's behavior while keeping his promise and staying the course of forgiveness and love.

What of us? You and I rejoice in the Lord's Resurrection, as the holy women did. Surely we are invited by our Gospel this evening to be tellers of the resurrection to our generation as they were to theirs! Surely this broken and terrorized world of ours needs some news of resurrection and new life! Surely we know people in our community with a good education and a good job and good prospects—and a sense of going nowhere in terms of their souls! And those in their sunset years—what of them? Each of us knows a relative or an acquaintance in the evening of life who does not know what to do with, or where to bring, their heart's filing cabinet of disappointments and collapsed dreams. And what of the young—losing idealism, losing meaning, losing touch?

What of all of these? Will we be the tellers of the joyful news that the Lord's Resurrection is also their invitation to newness of life? And will we be the interpreting angel who points out what is missing in the social scenario around them and, more so, in the personal scenario within them, and who leads them to see new possibilities in their lives by seeing the tomb and its transcendence in Christ's own?

# Easter

# 42ABC Easter Sunday

**The Resurrection of the Lord**
**The Mass of Easter Day**

## JOHN 20:1–9

### An Empty Tomb

The worth of our lives as Christians relies on the event we call the Resurrection of our Lord. As Saint Paul puts it, "And if Christ has not been raised, then empty is our preaching; empty, too, your faith" (1 Corinthians 15:14). Because of this dependence of our faith on the Resurrection, the apostles are at pains to show us that Jesus truly rose from the dead and that he plainly showed himself to them and to many others after his Resurrection.

The beginnings of that telling are here in this Gospel reading today. John tells us that Mary of Magdala is astonished to find the stone rolled back, and Matthew tells us why in his version of the Resurrection (see Matthew 27:66). The authorities had sealed the stone in place and had placed hand-picked temple guards over it. In other words, neither Mary of Magdala nor the apostles could have stolen the body. Peter is amazed to find the tomb empty, and John notices the neat arrangement of the linen cloths and the headcloth, a neatness that grave-robbers would not bother with. The cloths are lying there, as biblical scholar William Barclay puts it, "in their regular [burial] folds as if the body of Jesus had simply evaporated out of them" (*Daily Study Bible: John*, Nashville, TN: Westminster John Knox Press, 2001).

The Gospel's presentation of the Resurrection is very deliberate. It wants to assure us that our faith does not rest on fiction, nor on faith alone, but on fact.

Over the next few weeks in the liturgy, the readings will present us with additional "proofs" or "showings" of the Lord's Resurrection. All of this is done to cement our faith in Jesus and to inspire us to follow the Lord—as the words of *Godspell* have it—"more clearly, more nearly, and more dearly."

Saint Paul calls Jesus the "firstborn from the dead" because of the Resurrection (Colossians 1:18). Now we, by grace, are attached to Jesus, so that what happened to him will happen to us. We are, then, the subsequent births of the Resurrection. We will be raised up in glory on the last day. Paul writes, "For just as in Adam all die, so too in Christ shall all be brought to life, but each one in proper order: Christ the first fruits; then, at his coming, those who belong to Christ"; (1 Corinthians 15:22–23).

But first, we must follow the pattern set for us by Christ. We must rise from our present tombs as he rose from his. We must allow ourselves to be raised from our tombs by grace and through our cooperation with grace. What might these tombs be? We know what Jesus' tomb was, and what put him there. What about our own tombs? What put us in them? And why might some of us still be in them or only halfway out of them?

Our tombs are as varied as the vagaries of the human heart. Our tomb may be our consuming self-pride. Or it may be the tomb of excessive drinking. It may be the tomb of drug addiction. It may be the tomb of a violent or an abusive relationship, or the despair of ever "coming out." It may be the tomb of fear, in the sense that we are so accustomed now to our particular tomb that we are afraid someone may come along (a missioner, a therapist, or a friend) and roll back the stone and expose us to the challenge of living a fully committed Christian life.

In Matthew's version of the Resurrection, the angel says to Mary of Magdala, "Do not be afraid!" (28:5); the words are spoken to us too. Do not be afraid! Do not be afraid to leave whatever tomb still holds you. Do not be afraid of following your Lord in the power of his Resurrection grace. You do not have to continue celebrating Easter with, as it were, one foot still in your tomb, thereby receiving less than the full measure of the Easter joy that the Lord wants you to have.

But Jesus can't do everything for us. A little cooperation on our part is necessary. And so, Blaise Pascal, the brilliant mathematician, inventor, and mystic, puts the following words on our Lord's lips, and he intends them for you and for me if, on this glorious Easter morning, we should still be hugging our tomb out of fear and not making the small personal effort needed to cooperate with Easter grace. We must visualize Jesus saying to us: "Be comforted. I thought of you in my agony. I shed those drops of blood for you. . . . But do you want me always to pay with the blood of my humanity without your shedding even a single tear?" (*Pensées — Thoughts on Religion*, translated by A. J. Krailsheimer, New York: Penguin, 1994).

# 44B Second Sunday of Easter

## Divine Mercy Sunday

## JOHN 20:19–31

### The Lone Ranger

Faith is in crisis in much of the Western world. It is in some measure of difficulty here at home, too. The numbers generally aren't what they used to be, and certainly not as a percentage of world population growth. The Catholic commentators I read generally worry about our lack of knowledge of the faith, and therefore about our ability to pass it on to the next generation. (See, for example, Peter Steinfels, *A People Adrift,* New York: Simon & Schuster, 2003.)

Today's Gospel does not address the issue of Church growth and enlargement as such but it does have something to say about it in an indirect way. Today's Gospel can be read as a "preventive" gospel, as a gospel encouraging us to help people whose faith is weak. In this way, we may help forestall their falling away. We may not enlarge the Church by attending to this Gospel reading today, but we may help prevent its further contraction.

Before we look at this Gospel, we may allow ourselves a measure of comfort. We should realize that the decline in faith is not, actually, peculiar to our country or our time and generation. Faith, throughout the Western world, has been declining for several hundred years. The decline did not begin with the Second Vatican Council, or with the Beatles, or in the 1990s! For example, the poet Matthew Arnold expressed his personal anguish over the decline of faith as long ago as the mid-nineteenth century in his poem, "Dover Beach," where he laments the "melancholy, long, withdrawing roar" of the "Sea of Faith."

Today's Gospel has a suggestion for you and me in relation to those who are weak in faith, especially if they are family members, friends, or fellow workers who may be in danger of becoming unchurched. The Gospel suggests that Thomas, a hand-picked apostle, became weak in his faith and then did the worst thing possible: he left the company of the apostles. He left the company of his fellow believers. "He sought loneliness rather than togetherness," suggests scripture scholar William Barclay. He went off on his own with his difficulties, whatever they were, and they became his doubt. In acting this way, he moved further and further away from Christ and from the companionship of the apostles. He moved away from contact with the critical support blocks of his faith.

Beware of becoming a Christian Lone Ranger!—trying to live the faith on your own. And try to dissuade any fellow- or sister-believer from becoming a Christian Lone Ranger. Our hold on the faith relies to a great degree on the hold that the faith community has on us and on our involvement in the faith community. Thomas had, it seems, become a Lone Ranger. Is this the reason why he was not with the apostles the first time Jesus came to the house?

The other apostles, apparently, sought out Thomas. They must have spent long hours supporting him and encouraging him and trying to resurrect his faith. They probably had to put up with what we ourselves have to put up with in our faith-fights with our children and friends: stubbornness, negativity, unreasonable demands. But they stayed with it and, because of that, Thomas's "I will not believe" began to break down. It became "I will believe if . . . ." Next, we find that Thomas was present with the apostles when Jesus came the second time to the house.

It is important that we stay with the weak in faith in order to help them remain connected. It is important that they stay connected with the family of faith, with the community of believers, with the parish. The author of the letter to the Hebrews is concerned with this very issue of Christians drifting away from the faith even in the first generation after Christ. "Let us hold fast," he writes in the New Oxford Annotated Bible version, ". . . not neglecting to meet together, as is the habit of some" (Hebrews 10:23, 25). The New American

Bible version reads, "We should not stay away from our assembly, as is the custom of some . . ." (Hebrews 10:25). Meeting? Assembly? These words mean that the text is stressing the need for Christians to be active members of the faith community and to be present at the Eucharistic liturgy! Otherwise, they will weaken in their faith. It is a text for our times.

The Lone Ranger type of Christian is at risk in any generation and especially in our own as we move from centuries of faith to unsure secularism. In the phrase of historians Will and Ariel Durant, we are becoming an "unmoored generation" (*The Lessons of History*, New York: Simon & Schuster, 1968). It is important, then, that we lovingly and intelligently support those who are weak in faith, and all who doubt as Thomas did. And it is important that the parish be known as a genuine community where one always finds loving and intelligent support.

So, let us try to make our parish as communitarian and as supportive as possible. This is our best hope for achieving some measure of the smallness, the companionship, the intimacy, and the one-on-one exchange which characterized the early Christian communities and which, illustrated by today's Gospel story about Thomas, either prevents Lone Rangers from forming in the first place or, if they do, calls them quickly in from the cold.

# 47B Third Sunday of Easter

## LUKE 24:35–48

### The Scandalous Messiah

The twenty-fourth chapter of Luke's Gospel, from which today's reading is taken, begins with the Resurrection and ends with the Ascension. In between there are two "showings" or resurrection appearances of Jesus. The first is to the disciples on the road to Emmaus; the second is to the apostles in the upper room in Jerusalem. You will notice that, in the Resurrection story and in the two appearances in today's Gospel, the profile of the Messiah as a messiah who had to suffer and die takes center stage. Why?

The Jews expected a glorious messiah and, with him, the start of a glorious earthly kingdom. But what did Jesus turn out to be? He turned out to be a suffering messiah who said that the kingdom was not of this world. The apostles had to deal with this "scandal." It was an ongoing issue for them in their efforts to persuade people that Christ was the Messiah. The Jews, in general, wouldn't buy it. Neither would the Greeks, for Paul also came up against it in his preaching to them: "We proclaim Christ crucified, a stumbling block to Jews and foolishness to Gentiles" (1 Corinthians 1:23).

In the Jewish view, the true messiah is a king like David. He rules a political kingdom of power and glory in this world as well as one of justice and peace—with the Jewish nation at its center. They could not see this messiah in Jesus. They felt that the apostles were abusing the scriptures, trying to change the messianic expectation by cobbling onto it the image of someone called the "suffering servant." The "suffering servant" is found in the book of Isaiah (ch. 53 especially). The Jews felt that the apostles were presenting their Messiah-Jesus in this suffering light simply because Jesus' life—as it turned out—fit that image. But, to the Jews, the one known as the suffering servant in Isaiah is not the messiah, and was never meant to be. He is, as an individual or as a corporate entity, someone else. Jesus, on the other hand, tells the apostles that the true messiah is a messiah who must suffer, die, and rise from the dead in order to fulfill all the messianic prophesies. Jesus says, in effect, that the popular expectation is too narrow, too selective, too political, and too geared to glory in this world. He is also saying—to us—that suffering and the cross, in our lives as in his, are central to salvation.

And so, Paul goes to the Gentiles and says, "We proclaim Christ [as a Messiah] crucified" (1 Corinthians 1:23). And he insists that as true believers all of us must identify with the cross of Jesus, accepting the cross into our lives in whatever form it enters them, because "we are afflicted, . . . perplexed, . . . persecuted, . . . struck down, . . . always carrying about in the body the dying of Jesus, so that the life of Jesus may also be manifested in our body. For we who live are constantly being given up to death for the sake of Jesus, so that the life of Jesus may be manifested in our mortal flesh" (2 Corinthians 4:8–11).

Carrying our share of the cross of Christ is an anachronism to the modern mind and to much contemporary religion. It does not resonate with the current social vision, priorities, feel-good interests, and earth-bound values. It's all so counter to the spirit of the age! It is meaningless and it is futile! Perhaps this is one reason why the Christian religion suffers decline today. It just does not fit the shape of modern society and the "good life" culture.

Perhaps it is also the reason why many people still regard Jesus highly but will not actually commit to him. His cross stands in the way. It stood in the way long ago for Jew and Gentile. Pain is the great modern no-no, and the theology of the cross is a bridge too far for our time. And yet, is it not a fact of life that every life has its cross, whether one is a believer or not, and that there is no immunity in this world from it for anyone? Should it, then, be all that difficult to accept the reality of the cross in our lives, and instead of cursing it to name it our participation in the cross of Christ, and so turn our cross into an instrument of grace?

And in the matter of Christ crucified, is it really all that difficult to see Jesus as the true Messiah precisely because he was not a king of earthly splendor, with a kingdom of earthly splendor, for a people with earth-bound hearts and ambitions? In a Messiah crucified for his people, is it not easier to see the Messiah's dedication to his task and the depth of his commitment to us, and to sense what Paul calls "the breadth and length and height and depth" of Christ's love "that surpasses knowledge" (Ephesians 3:18–19)?

Scripture scholar William Barclay says, "The cross . . . was not an emergency measure when all else had failed and when the scheme of things had gone wrong. The cross was [always] part of the plan of God, for it is the one place on earth, where in a moment of time, we see his eternal love" (*Daily Study Bible: Luke,* Nashville, TN: Westminster John Knox Press, 2001).

If anyone is scandalized by the kind of Messiah Jesus turned out to be, he or she is scandalized by love.

# 50B Fourth Sunday of Easter

## JOHN 10:11–18

### The Good Shepherd

Somewhere I read that the image of the Good Shepherd is the image
most preferred by Christians for their Lord. I do not know if this
is so simply because the image is a non-threatening one, or because
Christians are able to find "the substantial Christ" in it. At any rate,
there's nothing soft about a shepherd who lays down his life for us, but
there is everything engaging about a shepherd who knows each of us
by name.

  The background of this speech by Jesus on the Good Shepherd
is his conflict with the Pharisees. He puts himself forward as the
"good" (more accurately, the "model") shepherd of God's people: the
Pharisees are mere hirelings. Jesus will bring God's "other sheep"
into the fold as well: the Pharisees insist on excluding them. These are
the Gentiles. The true friends of God recognize Jesus' voice; i.e., his
religious authority: they do not recognize the voice of the Pharisees.
He will lay down his life for God's flock: the Pharisees only scatter it
to the winds and the wolves.

  Our Lord must have really riled the Pharisees with this speech
because, while he speaks, they react violently to him. They tell the
people that he is possessed by a devil (v. 20), they reach for rocks to
stone him at least twice (v. 31), and they try to arrest him at least twice
(v. 39). Because of this violent reaction on their part and his with-
standing of it, one can appreciate how central the self-portrait of the
Good Shepherd is to Jesus—and how close he holds us, his flock,
to his heart.

  Because of this love of the Good Shepherd for his flock, it
is very sad to see so many people in our cities and towns (all dutifully
baptized, communioned, and confirmed) who no longer follow his
voice or lean on his love. It is sad to see them—the "crowds without
company" in Edward Gibbons's phrase—search in drink and drugs
and wild weekends for some form of replacement shepherding that

will ease their spiritual emptiness and anchor their loneliness. "All the lonely people, where do they all come from? All the lonely people, where do they all come from?" the Beatles ask repeatedly in "Eleanor Rigby." I think I could tell him. Most of them come from where they left—the Lord's side.

There's an unnecessary tragedy in this contemporary scene of the "crowds without company" on one side of the street of life, and Jesus, longing for their company, on the other side. There is a great thirst for love and belonging in both of them: in them to find it and in him to give it. If only they would see Jesus as the English diarist George Adam Smith saw the shepherd on the Judean plateau:

> On some high moor across which at night the hyenas howl, when you meet him, sleepless, far-sighted, weather-beaten, armed, leaning on his staff and looking out over his scattered sheep, everyone of them on his heart, you understand why the shepherd of Judea sprang to the front in his people's history; why they gave his name to the king and made him a symbol of providence; why Christ took him as the type of self-sacrifice.

Commenting on this, Barclay says, "This is the picture Jesus drew of God." But it is, I think, even more so the picture Jesus drew of himself. It is the picture of the shepherd so in love with his flock that they occupy his every living moment and even his death. If only the "crowds without company" would realize that they are always on his mind!

You and I pray that the Good Shepherd will never have to go out on the hills and into the gullies looking for us. And we pray, equally, that the "crowds without company" will allow themselves to listen to his voice and to be found by him, so that they may be lavished with love and carried home in joy on his shoulders.

# 53B Fifth Sunday of Easter

## JOHN 15:1–8

### Christ and Nominal Christianity

A casual reading of the Gospels hides the intensity of the struggle between Jesus and the religious establishment of his day, particularly the Pharisees. There was ongoing and often bitter rivalry between the two for the minds and hearts of the people. Jesus frequently takes revered images from the Jewish scriptures and, in disowning the religious establishment of these images, applies them to himself. In the process, he increases their antagonism toward him, and sets himself up for constant trouble and, eventually, the cross.

One of these revered images is the image of the true vine. Israel understood itself to be the true vine of God, and the religious establishment saw itself as the life force of that vine. But this true vine that God planted so lovingly long ago has come to "languish" (Isaiah 24:7) and to yield "wild grapes" (Isaiah 5:4). According to Jesus, this pastoral tragedy has occurred because of the uncaring and uncultivating hands of the religious establishment. He, therefore, dismisses them. In their place he puts himself. He is the true vine. In this way, he is presenting himself, says the Irish scholar Michael Mullins, "as the authentic source of life, light, nourishment, instruction and empowerment" (*The Gospel of John*, Blackrock, Co. Dublin: Columba Press, 2004).

In today's Gospel, Jesus solemnly affirms before the apostles what he has most likely stated before in public for the religious authorities to hear: "I am the true vine." And only those who follow him are "the branches" of the true vine. At this particular time in salvation history, you and I are the branches. How blessed we are!

Jesus says that the branches must adhere to the vine. We must adhere to Jesus, to his "life, light, nourishment, instruction and empowerment," so as to bear the fruit that his Father expects of us. Jesus makes it clear that without him we will produce nothing for the Father. A head of wheat will not develop, an ear of corn will not grow, and a flower will not bloom if they are cut off from their root. If there are Christians today who produce very little, is it not because they do not adhere to the vine in a meaningful way? What measure of productivity can be expected of Christians whose attachment to Christ is merely nominal?

Nominal Christians may be said to be Christians who are taken to church for Baptism at the start of life and taken there for a funeral liturgy at the end of life, but their life in between does not adhere in a meaningful manner to Christ and his Gospel but to the spirit of the world and its gospel. Jesus says that a genuine Christian is someone who adheres to him all the time, and cannot do otherwise. Nominal Christians languish on the vine, so to speak, and, at best, produce only "wild grapes" (Isaiah 5:4).

All Christian churches today have many such nominal members. These members are, again so to speak, half-in and half-out of their churches. Yet, most of us describe ourselves as Christians in the various polls and demographic surveys. But if most of us are Christian, why does social life not better reflect it? There is still much selfishness and anti-social behavior in society. Perhaps part of the answer has to do with deficiencies in early religious education and the relative lack of later adult Christian formation. Perhaps another part of the answer has to do with lack of motivation, and with not being open so as to be seized by the Spirit of God. At any rate, it is hard to align much in contemporary social behavior and in personal behavior with Jesus' vision of the kingdom of God on earth and all his followers as the branches welded to him, the vine. In the face of so much nominal Christianity today, G. K. Chesterton's observation is still largely valid: "The Christian ideal . . . has not been tried and found wanting; it has been found difficult and left untried" (*What's Wrong with the World*, San Francisco: Ignatius Press, 1994).

Today's Gospel has another level, which is deeper than the invitation to ethical rectitude that I have been outlining thus far. The Gospel of the vine and the branches is part of the Lord's last discourse, or "Parting Message" to his friends (as James McPolin puts it in *John: New Testament Message*, Collegeville MN: Michael Glazier, 1993). The theme of the parting message is love and our union with Christ in love. The Christian law of love is not primarily a set of ethical demands but a way of living in union with Christ. In this context, the parable of the vine and the branches is Jesus' invitation that we and he love the other intensely, and as two engrafted as one. How distant are so many contemporary Christians from this divine engrafting, languishing as they do in the shadowlands of nominal Christianity!

# 56B Sixth Sunday of Easter

## JOHN15:9–17

### Friends

One morning I drew back the drapes in my office and found a man sitting on a flower pot in my back patio. I recognized him as a transient who seemed to live his life just hitch-hiking up and down the local state highway. I knew him mostly from small talk about football and sports during rides in my car when he thumbed me down on the road. I knew something was up. Maybe he needed a ride to the city and wondered if I might be going there that day.

"How long have you been sitting here?" I asked him. "A long time," he said. "I didn't want to disturb you." I suspected that something serious was up. "What's troubling you?" I asked, scanning his face for the sign of illness or accident. "I tried to do away with myself," he said. We talked a long time over coffee. It took me by surprise when he said that he came to me because I was his friend.

In today's Gospel, Jesus says, "I no longer call you slaves [servants], but friends." Bible scholar William Barclay tells us, in his *Daily Study Bible: John* (Nashville, TN: Westminster John Knox Press, 2001), that both of these words—*servant* and *friend*—need to be understood as our Lord most likely understood them. They do not represent opposites but levels of proximity to the divine.

Among the ancient Hebrews, the slave or the servant of God was "a title of the highest honor." For example, David was God's servant and yet he was "the anointed of God" (Psalm 89:20). The early Christian community followed this Hebrew theology. That is why

Saint Paul begins his letter to Titus by naming himself "a servant of God" (1:1) and why James opens his letter with the same designation (1:1). "Servant" is an honorable title, even a mark of favoritism with the Lord. So, in elevating his apostles from the status of servants to that of friends, Jesus is not lifting them up from an inferior status but signaling an even greater honor and a closer proximity to the divine.

Again, Barclay explains how we may understand the meaning of "friends" as Jesus applies the term to his apostles. At the court of the Roman emperor there was a select group of men known as "the friends of the emperor." At all times, day or night, they had the right to enter the emperor's presence. No one else had such a right—no senator, no consul, no military commander. The emperor consulted "the friends" before he spoke with his statesmen or generals on any issue whether that issue was a matter of state or of military strategy. "The friends of the emperor were those who had the closest and the most intimate connection with him."

This is the context in which Jesus spoke of his apostles as his friends. Today, we meet Christians who have little or no appreciation of themselves as the servants of God as I have just described God's servants. They are still in the grip of religion as rule and regulation and of God as a master sergeant or a meticulous bookkeeper. And they have little or no understanding either of their vocation as the friends of God's beloved Son as Barclay described these friends. "What a friend we have in Jesus!" exclaims an evangelical hymn. If fearful Christians would see Jesus as their friend and themselves as his friends, their fears would fade, their hearts would fill, and their religion would become the joy that our Lord wants it to be. That we are called to be Christ's friends is not a platitude: it is our Christian vocation.

# 58B The Ascension of the Lord

## MARK 16:15–20

### A Theology of Hope

Our faith is a gift and a task. It is an unspeakable gift from God to us.
It is a holy task we are called to do. We are called to live the life of
faith and to invite others to share in the life of faith. Our faith touches
the core of us and it fulfills us deeply.

At the present time we may find living the life of faith a little
more challenging than in the past. I want to encourage us to stay
the course. Today's feast of the Ascension of our Lord is a wonderful
reason why we should stay the course. At the end of his life of faith
and service, the Lord Jesus was taken up into glory. That, dear friends,
is our future too. It is our "horizon of hope" at this time.

Being a child of the Second World War, perhaps like many
of you, I have read my share of war novels and histories. War books
are usually pretty torrid things, but they are never without aspects
of the good and even of the heroic. If war brings out the worst in some
people, it brings out the best in others. I think it is the combination
of the good and the heroic, set against the background of the torrid
that has helped me to keep my balance in life and to counter its deeper
troughs. The abject misery of the people in these war books only
forces me to count my own blessings, and give thanks to God for all
I have.

Among my greatest blessings is my faith. Since my faith is
inextricably tied up with the Church, I must name the Church among
my greatest blessings, too. The two of them—my faith and my
Church—give me my horizon of hope at this time, and at all times.
The two of them will carry me, under God's grace, to glory. They will
do the same for you too.

I find myself, then, not lacking the horizon of hope at all
as I look at my Church in this challenging time. Besides, I realize that
the Church is in good hands because it is in Christ's hands. But the

Church is not only a gift that the Lord has given us; it is also a care upon our hearts and a responsibility on our shoulders.

One of the Second World War's heroes of Christian resistance to the Nazis was the young Lutheran theologian Dietrich Bonhoeffer. He was arrested by the Nazis in 1943, interned in Buchenwald concentration camp, and hanged at Flossenburg concentration camp just a few weeks before the war ended. The Nazis would not let him go even when they knew that their regime was finished. They had a very old score to settle with Bonhoeffer—he had been one of their earliest critics. I am always impressed by what a Christian of heroic stature has to say about the Church because I know it doesn't come out of a book, or from blind loyalty, but from the depth of that person's soul. Of the Church, Bonhoeffer had this to say: "The Church is . . . not very influential, not a very imposing institution, and always in dire need of improvement." Nevertheless, he added, "The Church is an office from God" ("What Is the Church?" in *No Rusty Swords* Nashville, TN: Abingdon Press, 1977).

In our time, you and I may well say likewise: the Church is not a very imposing institution, and it is in dire need of improvement. But we must not stop there, forgetting the most important thing that Bonhoeffer said about the Church: "The Church is an office from God." By office, he meant that the Church is a care we have from God, and a work to be done for the Lord and for the salvation of others. Today's Gospel reading says, "The Lord worked with [the apostles] and confirmed the word" through them. Similarly, the Lord works with his Church in our time and in its difficulties, and he confirms his message through the Church's liturgy, word, and sacraments; through its teachers and preachers, its prophets and saints; and even—praise God!—through you and me.

Let us never lose the horizon of hope! Today's Gospel is a theology of hope for the Church and for us. Jesus ascends to glory at the end of his life on earth. He has spent his life showing us how to find meaning and purpose and joy through a life of faith in him and a life of service to others. He has shown us how to live with the horizon of hope ever before our eyes. He has told us that glory is the reward of such a faith-filled, servant life.

As he lived, may we live. And as all ended in glory for him, so may all end in glory for us. This is not a vain hope for a vague future.

It is the actual future of which Jesus is the real-life pattern, and of which his Ascension is the pledge.

# 60B Seventh Sunday of Easter

## JOHN 17:11B–19

### The War of the Worlds

For all its flaws, our world is a wonderful place. "The world is charged with the grandeur of God," writes Gerard Manley Hopkins in his poem "God's Grandeur." "The earth is the Lord's and all it holds, the world and all who live there. For God founded it on the seas, established it over the rivers," writes the Jewish psalmist (Psalm 24:1–2). "God created the world according to his wisdom," says the *Catechism of the Catholic Church* (#295). This world, says Saint Francis of Assisi, was "formed in heaven." In today's Gospel, Jesus says that he is not of the world, and neither can we be. Clearly, the world that Jesus despises and that he warns us against cannot be the world that we have just described, the world of God's grandeur, formed in heaven. What world then is Jesus condemning? We find the answer in John 16:8–11. There the Holy Spirit is said to convict the world of its sin, and to condemn it for not accepting Christ. Hence, the convicted and condemned world is the unbelieving and sinful world that stands apart from Christ.

For sure it's the world of the great military tyrants and thugs of history, but it is also the world of grasping and of economic greed, of exploitation and marginalization that disguises its sin under the pleasing language of development and progress.

The convicted and condemned world is also the world of terror in our streets, the world of snipers and serial killers, of knives and baseball bats and mugging and maiming, the world of abortion and euthanasia, of drugs and stupefied drinking, of reckless driving and road rage, and the hundred other pagan behaviors that mark so many today as people "apart from Christ."

The convicted and condemned world can be as active in the high political and financial places, and along the corridors of power, as on the meanest of city streets and back alleyways. Scripture scholar William Barclay calls the convicted and condemned world "human society organizing itself without God" (*Daily Study Bible: John*, Nashville, TN: Westminster John Knox Press, 2001).

But the world cannot successfully organize itself without God! That is the lesson of history. And the human person cannot organize himself or herself without grace! That is the lesson of our mean, modern streets. "There is no significant example in history," write the historians Will and Ariel Durant, "of a society successfully maintaining moral life without the aid of religion" (*The Lessons of History*, New York: Simon & Schuster, 1968).

When the world stands apart from Christ it cannot progress. It cannot even preserve its sanity, for it comes under the influence of the evil one. So says Jesus in verse 15 of today's Gospel reading: "I do not ask that you take them out of the world but that you keep them from the evil one." It collapses under Satan's influence. The proof is all around us today. And history is ragged with the same proof. Therefore, in today's Gospel, Jesus prays to his Father for his disciples— and for us. He prays that we will abide in him. He prays that we will stand up for the world as the Father created it, as a good and gracious thing. He prays that we will stand for a world reformed and renewed in his precious blood. He prays that we will stand for the world that is guided by the Spirit in goodness. And he prays that the other world, the world of the evil one, the world apart from him, the convicted and condemned world, the world organizing itself without God, will not contaminate and corrupt us.

In order that we may advance the world that stands with Jesus, he tells us that he has passed on to us the gift that he received from the Father. What is the gift? It is the knowledge of what is true and false in this life, and the wisdom to be able to distinguish the good from the bad. And it is the grace of doing the right and avoiding the wrong. So long as time endures, the struggle will go on between the better world and the blighted world. Both worlds and both worldviews have their supporters today as they've always had. Where do we stand? Our little moment in history is our chance to organize the world

along the lines of God's design, and our chance to oppose the building
of that warped world that stands apart from Christ.

# 62ABC Pentecost Sunday

## At the Vigil Mass

## JOHN 7:37–39

### Living Waters

The setting of our Gospel reading this evening is the Jewish Feast of
Tabernacles or *Sukkot*. This feast lasted eight days. It held great cultural
and religious significance for the people.

  The feast celebrated important aspects of Jewish life and
history. It occurred at harvest time and so, for one thing, celebrated
the ingathering of the harvest. An ancient Hebrew name for the
feast is the Feast of *Asip*—the Festival of the Ingathering. In ancient
times, as the harvest ripened, the people built temporary huts or
tents in the fields and vineyards as a protective measure. Hence, the
feast was also called the Feast of *Sukkot,* a word whose root meaning
is "protection" (Michael Mullins, *The Gospel of John,* Blackrock,
Co. Dublin: Columba Press, 2004). The phrase "Feast of Tabernacles"
comes from the original meaning of *tabernacle,* which is a temporary
dwelling or tent.

  In our Lord's time, during the eight days of the feast, the
people continued to leave their homes and to live in flimsy tents for
the duration. Even city dwellers, with no farming connections at all,
did this. The tents were made of willow branches and palm fronds
and they "sprang up everywhere, on the flat roofs of the houses, in the
streets, in the city squares, in the gardens, and even in the very courts
of the Temple" (William Barclay, *The Gospel of John: The New Daily
Study Bible ,Volume 1*. Nashville, TN: Westminster John Knox Press,
2001). In this manner, the people recalled the forty-year journey
of their ancestors, who pitched their tents each night and struck

them again each morning, during the Exodus from Egypt to the
Promised Land.

A central ritual of the Feast of Tabernacles involved water.
Each day of the festival the temple priest went to the Pool of Siloam
and carried a golden pitcher of water back through the Water Gate
while the people recited the words of the prophet Isaiah: "With
joy you will draw water at the fountain of salvation" (Isaiah 12:3). The
water was then poured into a perforated bowl, allowing it to flow over
the altar, while the people chanted the Hallel psalms (Psalms 113—
118). No doubt the people thus recalled the many aspects of their
history, which made them, as a desert people, so aware that water was
a supreme blessing in their lives. William Barclay suggests that it was
at this ceremony of water, on the final day of the festival, that Jesus
spoke his words, "Let anyone who thirsts come to me and drink.
Whoever believes in me, as scripture says, 'Rivers of living water will
flow from within him.'" (John 7:37–38).

What did the Lord wish his hearers to understand by his
words? They knew what *water* meant in the usual sense of the word
and even in its spiritual sense. But Jesus wanted them to understand it
in an entirely new—even radical—spiritual sense. The "living water"
is his own word and grace. This is the water by which—in Saint Paul's
phraseology—we now "live in newness of life" (Romans 6:4) and
through which we "lay hold of eternal life" (1 Timothy 6:12). One
cannot read these temple words of Jesus without recalling his parallel
words to the Samaritan woman at the well: "Whoever drinks the
water I shall give will never thirst; the water I shall give will become
in him a spring of water welling up to eternal life" (John 4:14).

Saint John, our Gospel writer, notes that the great
transforming action of Christ's word and grace on believers, a function
of the Holy Spirit, could not properly begin until Jesus had first
undergone Calvary and entered into his glory. This is the meaning of
the words "There was, of course, no Spirit yet." The Spirit only came
with boundless sanctifying power at Pentecost. Then was released fully
the torrent of living water; i.e., Christ's overflowing grace.

Dear friends: we are in the age of the Holy Spirit. It may seem
hard for us to believe this. But for all the terror and inhumanity that
still disfigures the human family, and that tends to depress our spirit at
times, be assured that the Holy Spirit is active and will see goodness

triumph over evil. Know, too, that the Spirit still inspires the human family to new insights and to new understandings; to the spread of the good heart and the gentle spirit and to better relationships; to most beneficial discoveries in the sciences and in medicine; and to new depths of beauty through the arts and of well-being through technology. And, finally, for all the backsliding we may be guilty of in our own life's journey, remain assured that in the Spirit all things are still possible. We may yet not only overcome our failings, but even become the saints God desires us to be.

# 63b Pentecost Sunday

## Mass during the Day

## John 15:26–27; 16:12–15

### Depending on Us

When Pilate asked Jesus what his mission on earth was he answered, "to bear witness to the truth" (John 18:37). Is the world really interested in the truth? I watched a TV program recently on the enormous influence that the "image makers" and the "spin doctors" have on the choices we make. It seems that, in our patterns of buying and voting, many of us are more influenced by image and presentation than by substance and truth.

The truth that Jesus came to bear witness to is "the truth of God." "The truth of God" is a phrase repeated over and over in the Old Testament in one form or another: God is a God of truth (Deuteronomy 32:4). God is true (Isaiah 25:1). God's works are truthful (Daniel 4:37). God's truth endures forever (Psalm 117:2). God forms a people to walk before him in truth (1 Kings 2:4). In the New Testament era, John, the Beloved Disciple writes: "The law was given through Moses: grace and truth came through Jesus Christ" (John 1:17). Clearly, the truth matters with God!

In our Gospel today, Jesus announces the sending of the Holy Spirit as one sent to serve the truth. When you and I learned the gifts of the Holy Spirit in our catechism, we saw that these gifts are very much concerned with "the truth of God," with understanding that truth, being counseled in it and through it, and making it a characteristic of our lives. The gifts of the Spirit are wisdom, understanding, counsel, fortitude, knowledge, prayerfulness, and reverence of the Lord.

These gifts of the Spirit allow us to understand much of the so-called mystery of life and to discern the right choices to be made and the good paths to choose in following the way of the Lord. The Holy Spirit draws us into the way of holiness—and holiness, we must keep reminding ourselves, is our fundamental vocation in life. So writes a great, early promoter of the liturgical renewal that we are now blessed with, Dom Odo Casel, OSB: "The more we let the Spirit guide us, the greater the power of God's eternal life to grow in us" (*The Mystery of Christian Worship* (Milestones in Catholic Theology Series), New York: Herder and Herder, 1999).

Jesus calls the Holy Spirit our Advocate (or Counselor) in following Jesus and in living our lives according to Jesus' way. He also calls him "the Spirit of truth." In regard to truth, Jesus gives the Spirit four identifiable roles. First, says Jesus, the Spirit will "testify to me." This means that the Spirit assures us, in our hearts, that Jesus is truly Messiah and Savior and animates us to respond accordingly with deep faith and love. Second, the Spirit energizes us to testify to others about Jesus ("you also testify to me"). The Spirit emboldens us to testify that Jesus is "the way and the truth and the life" (John 14:6). And we are grasped by a conviction of the Spirit that Jesus and his vision and values are the solution to what the philosophers grandly call "the human crisis" and ordinary folk call, more simply, the messiness of life.

Third, the Spirit guides us "to all truth." We must take the expression "all truth" to mean not only religious and saving truth, fundamental though these be, but also the many forms of truth/revelation embedded in God's creation and waiting to be uncovered and utilized. It is the Spirit who leads men and women to great beneficial discoveries in science, technology, and medicine, and who inspires the sublime music and poetry and the noble documents and charters by which humanity may live a decent and satisfying life. These forms

of revelation or truth are not yet exhausted. They are ongoing.
Needless to say, the vocation of uncovering all such truth is hindered
by greed and violence, neglect and abuse of nature and the environment.

Fourth, says Jesus, the Spirit tells us the truth about "the
things that are coming." Perhaps we should understand the "things
that are coming" not only as the terminal events of salvation history,
but also as the challenges that each Christian generation must
face in its own time and place. The Spirit, Jesus infers, tells us the truth
about our pastoral situation when we prayerfully read the signs of the
times, evaluate them in the light of the mind of Jesus, and act on them
with the heart of Jesus. This charism is a gift not only to the Church
in general, but to each one of us who is pledged to Christ and his way,
and who is happily open to the impulses of the Spirit of God.

Biblical scholar James McPolin writes: "All this work of the
Spirit in the life of the Christian is not just an intellectual communion
of doctrine. . . . His mission is to lead disciples more and more
into a life of personal communion with Christ, who is the truth.
Consequently, [the Holy Spirit] is a Spirit for Christian living" (*John:
A Biblical Theological Commentary*, Collegeville, MN: Liturgical
Press, 1993).

# Ordinary Time

# 65B Second Sunday in Ordinary Time

## JOHN 1:35–42

### Come and See Jesus!

Letting go of the reins is hard for many people. It is hard for parents and it is hard for bosses. It is hard to let go of whatever measure of influence or power our positions in life once gave us. Many of us do not take easily to becoming "yesterday's man" or "yesterday's woman." Being elderly, reasonably retired, and having had a good tenure as a manager doesn't seem to matter a whole lot.

You'd think that letting go of the reins would be hardest of all for someone like John the Baptist. After all, he is still a young man when he lets go of the reins. And he is a man of powerful talent and of magnetic influence. He has turned a whole nation his way. All the people regard him as a saint; some even as the Messiah himself. But in today's Gospel, he lets go and turns his followers over to Jesus without a moment's hesitation. It is as if he has been waiting for this moment all of his life.

As soon as he spots Jesus passing by, he says to his followers, "Behold the Lamb of God!" He might have added, "There is the One who takes away the sin of the world! This is the One whose sandals I am not worthy to untie! He is the One I've been preparing you for! Now follow him!"

Two of John's disciples approach Jesus. He asks, "What are you looking for?" They answer in the form of a question, "Where are you staying?" It means, "Where is the place you teach so that we may go there and learn from you?" Our Lord answers, "Come, and you will see." "Come and see" was a standard teaching device among the rabbis.

Scripture scholar William Barclay adds that, "When Jesus said 'come and see' he was inviting them not only to come and talk but to come and find the things that he alone could open out to them"

(*The Gospel of John: The New Daily Study Bible,* Louisville, KY: Westminster John Knox Press, 2001).

All of us have things that we need someone to "open out" for us. All of us have questions. All of us look for answers. All of us seek solutions. All of us want meaning in our lives. All of us need new purpose especially when—all too soon—we are yesterday's man and yesterday's woman and we see the shadows lengthen (to borrow Cardinal Newman's image for the closing of the day). Everyone needs the horizon of hope no matter what age or stage they're in.

Bumper-sticker theology tried to give the horizon of hope to the generation of the 1960s and 1970s. It was the time when parents despaired of their drugged and drop-out children, and the drugged and drop-out children despaired of their parents' priorities—the endless commuting and the mountain of material possessions. Between them, the parents and the children made up what a popular song called the going-nowhere generation. Then a blitz of bumper stickers confronted them with "Jesus Is the Answer." In today's Gospel, Jesus invites the present generation to beware of its cul-de-sac consumerism and its going-nowhere streets and instead, to "come and see" him.

I look at the same TV commercials and glossy magazine ads as you do. They are invitations to you and to me to enter the modern gallery of endless gadgetry and to define our lives in terms of possessions. The TV commercials and the magazine ads also invite us to Tarot card readings, to "the psychic zone," to palmistry and astrology. You may not take them seriously but, obviously, many among us do. After all, someone is paying for these constant ads so it must be an industry with a considerable clientele. Jesus, in today's Gospel, says to all of these purveyors and to their devoted clientele, "Come and see me instead!"

We are tired of the widespread drug addiction and alcoholism in our well-off and well-educated society that ought to know better. We are tired of the users and the abusers, the bullies and the bombers, the thugs and the terrorists who are hell-bent on organizing the world to suit themselves without reference to God or to decent citizens. They sorely need to hear the words of John the Baptist: "Look! There is the Lamb of God!" There is Jesus! There is the One who can take away your sin and your going-nowhere existence! He is your blueprint for a life that has meaning and purpose to it, and the blueprint for a society of love and peace and justice! Jesus and his values and his way of conducting life are the answer!

Cyril Connolly wrote in *The Unquiet Grave,* "We are all serving a life-sentence in the dungeon of self." Indeed we are, especially if by self we mean sinful self. Erich Fromm wrote, "Man's main task in life is to give birth to himself" *(Man for Himself).* And it is, if by giving birth we mean that men and women must come out of their cocoon of self-centeredness and fashion themselves into responsible and mature human beings. And where will they find the pattern and the grace to achieve that? Jesus says in today's Gospel, "Come and see."

# 68B Third Sunday in Ordinary Time

## MARK 1:14–20

### A Rendezvous with Destiny

The drifter is a staple of western movies. He is the silent and slow-moving stranger on the silent and slow-moving horse. It takes him a whole day to make a dent in the mileage before him. He moves as a distant speck through the dry, endless sagebrush of the New Mexico desert or disappears from our sight in the great green forests on the slopes of the snow-capped Rockies. The immensity of these landscapes intensifies his insignificance in this world.

The drifter relies on his horse to pick the patches of footing among the rocks and the gullies and to find the best slope of the bank on the far side of the river. The camera pans in on his weathered face and searches his sun-narrowed eyes. It challenges us to decode the drifter's past, and to wonder if he has a future. At sundown he drifts into an unnamed town—not knowing he has a rendezvous with destiny.

Today's Gospel places two very ordinary men in a small boat by the shore. Their background is the wide expanse of the Sea of

Galilee. Against this expanse of water they are specks. They are insignificant. They are doing what they have been doing since childhood. What they are doing is as insignificant as themselves— at least in the great design of the universe and in the priorities of the movers and the shakers of Israel. They are simply "casting their nets into the sea; they were fishermen." Their lives, like the lives of their fathers before them, seem destined to be book-ended by fish. But on this particular morning, all unknown to them, they have a rendezvous with a very different destiny. Jesus appears on the shore and calls to them, "Come after me, and I will make you fishers of men."

Bible scholar Wilfrid Harrington, in his commentary on Mark (*Mark: New Testament Message—A Biblical-Theological Commentary*, Collegeville, MN: Michael Glazier, 1979), tells us that Mark "shapes" this incident to "bring out the nature of Jesus' call and of the Christian response." The call is compelling; the response is immediate. The call is modeled on the call of Elisha who immediately breaks with his family and his life's occupation (see 1 Kings 19:19–21). Simon and Andrew likewise immediately leave their nets and their boats and fol- low Jesus. It is a free response. It is an immediate response.

It is a total response.

The brothers' lives and their work and their history are now split decisively into two chapters: what went before and what begins now; what was insignificant and what is to be momentous.

Mark also shapes the incident to bring out why Simon and Andrew followed Jesus without hesitation and, in Mark's telling of it, even without reflection. Harrington says, "the decisive factor is the person of Jesus himself." It is "the mighty impression of Jesus" on them. William Barclay says it is "the magnetism" of Jesus' eyes and his "tug on the heart." While all of this is true there may be an unrecorded preface to it. Simon and Andrew may already have heard Jesus preach by the shore or in their village and may have been already under his spell. If this is true then they were predisposed to follow him if ever he should call them. In today's Gospel the call is made and that is why it is immediately accepted.

Today's Gospel challenges us on our call and our response. We are ordinary people as Simon and Andrew were. We would be as insignificant as they once were had Christ not touched us as he likewise touched them. In the "gigantic flywheel of the universe" (H. L. Mencken's term) we may count for little more than the weight of an atom, as against the expanse of the Sea of Galilee the apostles once counted for as little as their ability to catch a few fish. But Christ has called us and given us primary significance in the universe and in the saving designs of God. He has chosen us for a new way of living in this world and for the extraordinary destiny that follows it. And he has called us to be "fishers of men" in our own generation so that as many as possible may lose their insignificance and abandon their drifting lives. For, in the words of Saint Paul, God "wills everyone to be saved and to come to knowledge of the truth." And the truth is this: "There is one God. There is also one mediator between God and the human race, Christ Jesus, himself human, who gave himself as ransom for all" (1 Timothy 2:4–6).

# 71B Fourth Sunday in Ordinary Time

## MARK 1:21–28

### The Main Man—and Others

It was one of those raging Southern California fires at the end of a long, hot summer. The brush was bone-dry and the fire ate through it at a speed you could actually see. The canyons funneled in air from the valleys to create mini firestorms, and the eucalyptus trees and the palm trees along the coast highway exploded like gasoline bombs. Ash fell miles away painting all the parked cars in the streets a deathly gray.

The fire stopped at the back wall of a parish church in Malibu. But the priests weren't too quick to claim divine intervention —because the previous fire had incinerated the rectory. Dozens of homes in the parish hills were lost. An older man was particularly distraught. He felt he hadn't the years left to rebuild. What bothered him most was the loss of the small things: childhood photos, mementos of war service, the love letters of his deceased wife when she and he were young. Trauma counseling was made available and a year of meetings began in order to organize our community better for the next time. By the end of the year the older, distraught man had emerged as a natural leader, and on him was placed the burden of parish coordination in future emergencies. He would be the "main man" in emergency situations.

Jesus emerges in today's Gospel episode as the people's "main man." Mark highlights the contrast between Jesus and the scribes who teach the people. God's word was to be found in the Torah, the first five books of the Bible, and God's word was binding for the people. Now its general principles were clear enough, but the application of these principles to the details of everyday living was not. It required a set of interpreters and teachers. It is this requirement that gave rise to the men known as the scribes.

Bible scholar Wilfrid Harrington speaks of the scribes as traditionalist and legalistic. William Barclay speaks of their fear of standing on their own authority when they interpret God's word for the people. Jesus, by way of contrast, "amazes" the people, for he speaks with great personal authority—and he offers the people what they describe as "a new teaching," viz. the proper and wholesome interpretation of God's word.

The people notice the contrast, too, between Jesus and the exorcists. He is victorious over the unclean spirits whereas the exorcists fail to unbind the possessed man. Jesus has that "supernatural aspect" (Harrington) which the others lack. In the eyes of the people there is Jesus and there are the others. The contrast between them is as sharp as that between day and night. From now on Jesus is their main man in everything to do with God, his word, and the living of their lives.

What of us? Who is our main man? We are an educated generation. We have a lot of knowledge, but have we wisdom? We are a skeptical generation. We question everything but commit whole-heartedly to very little. We are an ecumenical generation.

We know more than our parents did about others' deities but less, perhaps, about our own. We are the New Age generation. We visualize the dawning of the age of peace and harmony through the right conjunction of stars, or through the happy convergence of world religions rather than through God's Messiah who is God's blueprint and grace for the age of peace and harmony.

We are the star-struck and the celebrity-struck generation. The book that Oprah recommends on her TV show and the particular brand of deodorant that our favorite football stars endorse are immediate musts for our homes. Jesus, too, has a book. It is called the Good News of God. And he has bread. It is called the Eucharist.

So, here we are with Jesus and all these other guides and gurus in our lives. Who is our main man among them all? Who is our main man for the journey of life? And who is our main man for the passage from life that follows it?

# 74B Fifth Sunday in Ordinary Time

## MARK 1:29–39

### When They All Want a Piece of You

"Everyone is looking for you," they said to Jesus. It would be wrong to think that everyone in today's Gospel was looking for Jesus because of his message of salvation.

It would be wrong to think that everyone looking for him wanted a piece of him because they perceived him to be divine and they were enthralled with his message of the kingdom and his call to saving grace.

The truth is that everyone was looking for him because he was a wonder-worker and he could do things for them. Jesus' popularity in this Gospel incident is based on the curiosity of the crowd and on his novelty in their eyes. They want to hold on to him for their own purposes rather than for his. They want a piece of him because he has the cure. We can well understand the scene by comparing it with scenes that we might be familiar with ourselves. There is always a rush of people when someone in our own community is known to be a faith healer. We can understand the scene by comparing it with the buzz among people when the rumor of a new faith healer or of a new visionary begins to percolate in the community and everyone wants a piece of him or her.

The hard truth is that both the apostles and the crowd are, at this moment, the unwitting enemies of Jesus and of the divine plan. They are enemies "in the sense of attempting to turn him from his true mission" (Wilfrid Harrington, *Mark: New Testament Message— A Biblical-Theological Commentary,* Collegeville, MN: Michael Glazier, 1979). They are enemies in the sense that his mission is to proclaim the kingdom and to proclaim it to all of Israel and not just to one community. Luke, in his version of the same incident, says that the people would have prevented Jesus from leaving them if they possibly could (see Luke 4:43).

The first chapter of Mark, from which today's Gospel is taken, makes it clear that Jesus was always available to people in their legitimate need. One incident of his compassion and healing follows the other. Time and again the Lord gives a piece of himself to people as he goes from town to town proclaiming the good news and freeing people from their demons. And, although our Lord's humanity needs occasional relief from the stress of his mission and its hectic pace, he allows even these periods of rest to be interrupted time and again. But, always, the people's legitimate needs are responded to in the context of the preaching of the kingdom. Our Lord is simply not a fellow to flock to because "he is a healer."

Our own humanity, as our Lord's, requires periods of rest. We need our space. We need the chance to chill out. But, like the Lord (and like all the mothers of the earth) we should not press our rights when legitimate demands are made on us by others' need. Compassion must always be allowed to interrupt us. Our generation is often described as the "me" generation, as a selfish generation, but such a generation does not exist in the Christian lexicon. In Christianity, there can only be the generations of the "we."

In this Gospel passage we are introduced to the anchor and to the energy of the Lord's existence. The anchor and energy is his prayer life, his conversations with his Father. He just had to pray. He could not be forever giving and never receiving. What Jesus was doing in his prayer life was "summoning spiritual reinforcements to his aid"

(William Barclay). He was renewed by prayer. He was re-energized by prayer. And the longest periods of prayer came before the most critical events in his life. In his prayer he talks with the Father about the burning issues of his life and mission. And the Father responds by enlightening him and energizing him for these burning issues of his mission.

"What should I talk about in my prayer?" asks Saint Josemaría Escrivá in *Christ Is Passing By* (New York: Scepter Books, 1974). He answers, "The theme of my prayer is the theme of my life." So it was with Jesus. So it should be with us. The challenge before us then is to be generous in responding to the legitimate needs of others, and to be generous in serving them in the context of the kingdom of God on earth. We will find the energy for that generosity in a committed prayer life, and nowhere else.

# 77B Sixth Sunday in Ordinary Time

## MARK 1:40–45

### Christ's Leper and Ours

"Illness is the night-side of life," writes Susan Sontag in her book *Illness as Metaphor* (New York: Farrar, Straus & Giroux, 1978). In the time of our Lord, leprosy was the great illness, the great nightside of Jewish life. In fact, it was more. It was the great killer. It was the death-side of life. The lepers were the walking dead. It was only a matter of time until their disease finished them off.

Leprosy also finished them off in religious terms. Wilfrid Harrington, in his commentary (*Mark: New Testament Message— A Biblical-Theological Commentary,* Collegeville, MN: Michael Glazier, 1979), calls leprosy in our Lord's time "the ultimate uncleanness." Harrington states that it "cut-off the afflicted one from the community" lest that faith community suffer religious or ritual defilement. Hence, the New Testament does not describe the cure of leprosy as a healing but as a cleansing.

The Law could only "defend the community from the leper." It could do nothing for the leper himself. But Jesus changed all that.

Scripture scholar William Barclay, in his commentary on Mark, writes, "The leper was banished from the company of men. He must dwell alone outside the camp. He must go with rent clothes, bared head, a covering upon his upper lip, and as he went he must give warning of his polluted presence with the cry, 'Unclean! Unclean!' " (*Mark: New Testament Message—A Biblical-Theological Commentary*, Collegeville, MN: Michael Glazier, 1979).

The leper in today's Gospel had no right to be anywhere near Jesus (or anyone else) according to the Law. For that he risked both stoning and damnation. He risked his mortal life and his eternal life. What, then, drove him to seek out Jesus at such a massive risk to himself? We could say that, given his condition as one of the walking dead, the leper felt that any hope at all of a cleansing was worth any risk at all. But that doesn't strike me as a deep enough answer. It doesn't match the simplicity and the sheer faith and the few words of the leper. The man has childlike trust in Jesus' compassionate nature, and he has utter faith in his divine power. All he says to Jesus is, "If you wish, you can make me clean." Perhaps the leper, long before he set out to meet Jesus, already knew that the Lord's response would be, "I do will it. Be made clean."

Even though we have moved out of the age of leprosy, I think we still retain the social psychology that went with it. We still bring our community's fear and its social exclusion to bear on those individuals and groups that we do not like for one reason or another. Perhaps this Bible challenges us to name our modern-day lepers and to change our attitude from fear and exclusion to understanding and inclusion.

One of the sad and unintended consequences of the Second Vatican Council has been the division of the Church into camps, the liberals and the conservatives—or the prophetic and the orthodox, as they may see themselves. At any rate, the two camps have not yet lifted their mutual excommunications. And, after four decades, they do not seem to be in much of a hurry to do so. They remain theological lepers in each other's eyes.

Some of us, perhaps, hear our own hearts crying, "Unclean! Unclean!" when we come across people of color and "working poor" and even persons with special needs. The rash of broken marriages and failed relationships has created innumerable lepers in the hearts of people who once called these same lepers their loved ones. Years upon years of sectarianism in such places as Northern Ireland, Israel, Iraq, Afghanistan, and the Balkans have expanded the leper base on both sides of the religious divide (sometimes the Christian divide!) until it almost goes out of focus. We could go on and on. And the older we are the additional chances we have had of adding to our list of lepers. The flawed human heart seems to need its lepers because it needs its excuses.

Would you and I, instead, name the leper that is uppermost in our hate or in our pain today? And would we give that leper over to the Lord, so that he may heal our memory, mend our pain, and cleanse our heart?

# 80B Seventh Sunday in Ordinary Time

## MARK 2:1–12

### The Scribes' Problem and Ours

There is something deeply engaging about this scene of the men making a hole in the roof of the house where Jesus was. It's not something we would do. Can you imagine people taking the slates or the shingles off your house in order to let someone down to see you!

There is also something wonderful about the scene and that, surely, is the faith of the men who took off the roof and the faith of the paralytic who sought out Jesus. Making a hole in the roof was probably not as strange to the Jews as it would be to us. The typical Jewish roof was flat and it was made of timber and compacted earth.

It was easy enough to put up, and it would have been easy enough to punch through. When the men arrived at the house where

Jesus was, they found the place so packed with people that they could not even get near the door. So they went up on the roof, cut a hole in it, and lowered the paralytic down with ropes into the space where Jesus was. As we see in this Gospel scene—and in many parallel Gospel scenes—persistent faith is answered favorably by Jesus. He cures the paralytic and, for added measure, he forgives the man of his sins.

The scribes are shocked at our Lord's declaration, "Child, your sins are forgiven." Their reasoning is this: only God can forgive sin. No man, no matter how holy or how messianic, can do what only God can do. So they accuse Jesus of blasphemy. (This is the core charge that they will bring against him later when he is condemned to death.) To forgive sin is to try to take God's place. I suspect that this is the key reason why Jesus failed to convert the Jewish people to himself as Messiah, and to his Gospel, as the definitive Good News from God. He claimed the divine power of forgiving sin and, in their eyes, broke the very first commandment of the Law. "Hear, O Israel! The LORD is our God, the LORD alone!" (Deuteronomy 6:4).

Our problem is not that Jesus is able to forgive sin, or that he passed that power on to the Church, and that forgiveness is available to us in the sacrament of Penance or Reconciliation. Our problem is our loss of the sense of sin. We feel that we do not sin anymore, or if we do it's no big deal. When we lose the sense of sin and deny our sinfulness, we effectively reject Jesus as Savior, as the one who saves his people from their sins. Is this the reason why our generation scarcely uses the sacrament of Penance, God's forgiveness freely given, and why it does not seem to be able to identify in any deep sense with the meaning of the cross?

It is odd that we modern-day religionists have lost the sense of sin when non-religionists are very conscious of it. Albert Camus, the agnostic philosopher, observed sin in himself and in the people around him: "In the time of innocence I did not know that morality existed. I know it now." Ernest Becker, the psychologist, came to this conclusion from his long years of practice: "The plight of modern man: a sinner with no word for it." The one-time dean of American psychiatry, Karl Menninger, wrote a book late in his life with the title *Whatever Became of Sin?* These men had no problem locating sin in their work and in our lives. But we have such a problem. Why is that? Are we saints already, or are we just trying to con ourselves and God too? If you read

a newspaper, or watch the evening news on TV, or examine your conscience, you know that sin is alive and well.

That the scribes had a problem with Jesus as the forgiver of
sin doesn't surprise me all that much, given their sense of the absolute
uniqueness and otherness of God. That religionists like you and
I cannot see sin in ourselves in an age of chronic sin is another story.
We should acknowledge our sins and experience the joy of the paralytic who went so far as to go through the roof of a house in order
to hear Jesus say to him: "Child, your sins are forgiven."

# 83B Eighth Sunday in Ordinary Time

## MARK 2:18–22

### New Wine, New Skins!

The thought has sometimes struck me that the difference between
some of us and the saints is the difference between why? and why not!
We stand before the Gospel with a question mark: the saint stands
before it with an exclamation point. We ask why? at every Gospel
demand: the saint looks at each Gospel demand and says, why not!
What is a questionable demand in our eyes is an invitation to grace
and an opportunity of grace in the saint's eyes. That is why some
of us struggle to put on the Gospel while the saint wears it like a
tailor-fitted suit.

You will have noticed that the Gospels have several encounters
between Jesus and the people or the authorities in which the first
word out of their mouths is "why?" Yet they do not always ask "why?"
in a negative way, just to test Jesus or to stonewall him.

Sometimes their "why?" is an honest "why?" For it is, sometimes, part of the question-and-answer format that was the standard
learning methodology in Jewish religious education.

The people's "why?" in today's Gospel incident is an honest one. They ask Jesus, "Why do the disciples of John [the Baptist] and the disciples of the Pharisees fast, but your disciples do not fast?" Fasting was a feature of the life of every holy man and of his disciples. But Jesus and his disciples are not fasting. So the people, quite honestly, ask "why?"

In his response, our Lord invokes an image that the people are familiar with. No one, he says, fasts at a wedding banquet. On the contrary, they feast. Even the strict Jewish law dispensed the wedding guests from any scheduled fast falling on the wedding day, or during the celebratory days that followed. Jesus calls himself the bridegroom, and his disciples are the friends of the groom. They are what we today call the groom's attendants. In Jesus, there is the wedding of heaven and earth and, more specifically, the wedding of Jesus and the bride who is the embryonic Church.

We may understand the duration of Jesus' wedding feast to be the three years of his public ministry. These are years during which the Lord's disciples do not fast, for they are celebrating his presence among them. They feast on his word and they revel in his signs and wonders. These are years when they celebrate his divine presence as heaven comes down to earth. Saint John will later sum up the celebratory nature of these years with the line, "And the Word became flesh and made his dwelling among us, and we saw his glory, the glory as of the Father's only Son, full of grace and truth" (John 1:14).

But Jesus introduces a shadow over these happy proceedings. A day is coming, he says, when the bridegroom will be taken away from them. On that day they will fast. He is referring to his death. He is probably also referring to the persecution that his disciples will have to endure in future days when he is no longer with them. Those hard times to come will be times of fast, indeed.

Jesus, of course, is not against fasting as such. He uses the people's question about fasting as a springboard to deal with the more important issue of the true nature of religion. In the contrast between fasting and feasting, Jesus appears to disown the negative shape of traditional Jewish religion and to indicate the celebratory shape of his new kingdom religion. He makes a distinction between the two religions, between two very different understandings of religion, and between two very different approaches to God. He continues with this distinction when, later in this Gospel passage, he speaks of the new wine of his teaching being poured into new wineskins and not into the old skins of the Pharisees and scribes. They simply would not be able to contain it. You may recall that four Sundays ago the Gospel said that the people were "amazed at Jesus' teaching" (Mark 1:27). They found it to be "a new teaching with authority," because its emphasis and spirit were radically different from the emphasis and spirit of the theology of the Pharisees and scribes.

Jesus is, then, telling the people, through his answer to their question about fasting and through his heralding of new wine and new wineskins, that the messianic age has arrived. He comes with a message, as William Barclay says, "which is startlingly new" and with a way of life which is "shatteringly different from that of the orthodox rabbinical teacher." In the Lord's new religious order, fasting as such will not disappear, but fasting, so often done in the past to fulfill a legal requirement or to "look gloomy . . . so that they appear to others to be fasting" (as Jesus says in Matthew 6:16), will henceforth have the pure love of God behind it. The face of the new religion, and of the new believer, is the face of joy. For, in Christ, we have everything that matters and we are to become everything that matters.

Happy indeed are we in the kingdom of God, drinking the new wine of Jesus' teaching, grace, and joy.

# 86B Ninth Sunday in Ordinary Time

## MARK 2:23—3:6

### People over Rules

When I was a child I felt that the Lord's disciples sinned because they stole grains of wheat that didn't belong to them. I wondered why our Lord saw nothing wrong in it. I did not know that in those days, travelers were allowed to pluck the ears of someone else's grain in the fields by the roadside if they were hungry. They were allowed to do this even on the Sabbath. The Pharisees are misinterpreting the Sabbath law in attempting to condemn Jesus and his disciples for their action.

In rejecting the Pharisees' interpretation of the Sabbath law, Jesus quotes an incident from the first book of Samuel, chapter 21, verses 1 to 6. King David, God's anointed, and his men ate the holy bread of the temple—the "showbread"—when he and they were on the run and very hungry. Only the priests were allowed to consume this bread. Our Lord's first point is that human need is more important than rules and regulations. His second point is that the Sabbath is a gift from God to his people while the Pharisees have made it a rule-bound servitude.

In the incident of the man with the withered hand, Jesus repeats his teaching that human need is more important than rules and regulations. The Sabbath rest of the Pharisees may be broken in favor of human need. For the worship of God is reflected in helping people in their need as well as in Sabbath rest and in worship.

In today's Gospel scenes, Jesus puts himself forward as Lord over the Sabbath. He claims the divine right to interpret God's law, and he interprets it according to its spirit, in accord with God's great heart. He teaches that the law of love and of human need takes precedence over the lesser rules and regulations of religion. Or, as scripture scholar William Barclay puts it, "Whenever men forget the love and the forgiveness and the service and the mercy that are at the heart of religion and replace them by the performance of rules and regulations, religion is in a decline" (*Mark: New Testament Message—A Biblical-Theological Commentary*, Collegeville, MN: Michael Glazier, 1979). John P. Meier, in his commentary on the same incidents in Matthew's Gospel, invites us to consider these incidents in terms of the very nature of God himself. He writes: "The clash between Jesus and the Pharisees is fundamentally over the essence of God: is God to be conceived of in terms of legalistic will or liberating mercy?" (*New Testament Message: Matthew*, Collegeville MN: Liturgical Press, 1990).

Lest you think I am trying to make rules and rituals less important, I want to interject a thought at this point. As a worshipping people, we must not lose sight of the reason behind the many beautiful rituals we practice as part of our Catholic faith. It is in the Liturgy of the Eucharist where we come together as a community to worship our Creator in the words and rubrics that are fitting and proper ways to address God. We should also remember that in this same liturgy God addresses us, and speaks to us about our lives and our souls through the scripture and the important and sacred words of the ritual of the Mass. We need to remember the words and actions of the liturgies and how these rites support our human needs as worshipping beings.

The poet Carl Sandburg was aware of what ordinary people have to put up with in their sometimes less than adequate leaders and teachers. In his poem, "The People, Yes," he may have been thinking mostly of politicians when he wrote his lines, but they can be applied to all religious leadership and religious teaching, past or present, in the mold of the Pharisees. The people will live on, he said, no matter how short-changed or misled because they find their "rootholds" in the nourishing earth.

Jesus is the roothold of our faith and of our salvation. The teaching Church, and ourselves, must always be tapping into him as the roothold—into him, his word, and his spirit of religion—so as not to lose the spirit of the way.

# 89b Tenth Sunday in Ordinary Time

## MARK: 3:20–35

### Tell the Truth and Shame the Devil!

All nations exaggerate their victories and their heroes. All of their successful battles are "famous" victories, and all of their heroes acquire public personas that their mothers and their wives and their lovers might not recognize. Myth and mystique surround heroes. Memorable one-liners are attributed to them, which they may never have spoken at all.

It is said of the greatest of the English admirals, Horatio Nelson, that, at the Battle of Copenhagen in 1801, he didn't want to obey his commander's signal to disengage from the battle so he put his telescope to his blind eye and said, "I really do not see the signal." But Nelson was lying. He didn't want to face the truth.

In today's Gospel we have two groups who likewise do not want to face the truth. One group does not like the truth that Jesus may very well be the Messiah because it embarrasses them. This group is made up of family members. They actually set out to seize him and try to take him home because the neighbors are saying, "He is out of his mind." Why do they think he is out of his mind? He is out of his mind because he is challenging the powerful religious establishment and he will get himself and his family into trouble if he keeps it up. For this same establishment has seen and dismissed a thousand other would-be messiahs throughout the course of Jewish history. He is out of his mind—they think—because the demons are shouting, "You are the Son of God" as he expels them (v. 12), and he refuses to deny what the demons are saying of him. Jesus is embarrassing his relatives in front of the neighbors!

The second group that does not like the truth about Jesus is the group known as the scribes. These men were the theological experts of their day. Jesus is able to cleanse possessed people of their demons. Now the scribes cannot deny that he has this power over demons, for it is plain for them and for everyone else to see. But their reaction to Jesus' power is purely negative. Instead of thanking God that a son of Israel has been given so great a gift they say instead, "He is possessed by Beelzebul," the prince of demons, and it is "by the prince of demons he drives out demons" (v. 23).

The scribes are madly jealous of Jesus and his gift. They are threatened by him as well. For if Jesus really is the Messiah, their world and their jobs are about to come to an end.

Verse 29 introduces us to the sin that Jesus calls everlasting; i.e., unforgivable. He says, "Whoever blasphemes against the holy Spirit will never have forgiveness, but is guilty of an everlasting sin." What is this sin that is everlasting and unforgivable? It is called, variously, sinning against the light, or persisting in error when you know better, or "refusing the mercy and forgiveness of God" (*Catechism of the Catholic Church*, 1864), or—particularly—refusing to acknowledge Jesus as the Messiah.

Scripture scholar Wilfrid Harrington calls it "man's refusal of the salvation which God offers him through the Spirit active in Jesus" (*Mark: New Testament Message—A Biblical-Theological Commentary*, Collegeville, MN: Michael Glazier, 1979). It remains the one unforgivable and eternal sin in scripture unless, of course, one truly repents of it and comes into the light of the Spirit and to the forgiveness of Christ.

You and I are invited by this Gospel to examine ourselves with regard to our continuing acceptance of Jesus as the Messiah. We are also invited to examine ourselves with regard to the virtue of truthfulness. Are we truthful people? Or do we stretch the truth when it comes to defending ourselves and protecting our interests?

How readily do we go along with the exaggerations of others when they say that the neighborhood is "threatened" by a different "class" of people coming in, or threatened by the unemployment office where unemployed gather in the mornings, or by a halfway house for young runaways or homeless "half out of their minds"?

Are we more concerned about loyalty to friends and business associates and cronies when we should allow the truth to have its way and thus free them, in the long run, from their weaknesses and from their demons? Some people today, as yesterday, are not committed to the truth but to the cover-up.

Jesus said, "The truth will set you free" (John 8:32). What is the truth? Herbert Ager wrote, "The truth that makes men free is for the most part the truth which men prefer not to hear" *(A Time for Greatness)*. And it is. It is the truth of personal conscience that we do not want to hear. And it is the Gospel truth of Jesus that we do not always want to hear, but which must be allowed to shape our moral and religious life, our business and political life, and so preserve our life unto everlasting happiness.

In today's Gospel, Jesus and the truth find their enemies not only in the powerful establishment of the day but among close relatives and everyday "good" people. May Jesus and the truth never find additional enemies in us.

# 92B Eleventh Sunday in Ordinary Time

## MARK 4:26–34

### Is Goodness Growing?

These are two short parables about the growth of the kingdom of God. In the first parable, Jesus says that the kingdom is growing gradually but surely, even though we may not notice the growth. In the second parable, Jesus says that the presently small kingdom will become an immense one. The two parables form a theology of hope for our times.

What is the kingdom, or the reign of God? It has several levels and it has several stages of development. Let us take it to mean, primarily, the breaking in upon our hearts and upon the world of the rule and the grace of God. The kingdom already exists in the hearts of all who live committed Christian lives, lives of faithful obedience to God, and lives of love, peace, justice, and mercy. The kingdom is here already in them. And it will continue to spread and grow. And it will come to the fullness that God has predestined for it but only as history draws to a close. Is goodness, then, growing on the earth? Or is Jesus' kingdom and what he said about it just another utopian pipedream? It is a pipedream if you are someone who despairs of all the sin and violence on the earth. It is a pipedream if you read history the way some people do. For example, the novelist Lawrence Durrell said, "History is the endless repetition of the wrong way of living" (from "Alexandria and After: Lawrence Durrell in Egypt," *The Listener*, April, 1978). The historian Edward Gibbon called history "little more than the register of the crimes, follies and misfortunes of mankind" (*The Decline & Fall of the Roman Empire*, Chicago: NTC/Contemporary Publishing Company, 1999).

On the other hand, history can be read with "a brighter bias." The historians Will and Ariel Durant tell us that "history as usually written is quite different from history as usually lived." They mean that for every atrocious Hitler (who gets his crimes into the history books) there are millions of decent human beings (who do not get their good deeds into the history books). For what historian, ask the Durants, would "dare to write a history of human goodness?" (*The Lessons of History*, New York: Simon & Schuster, 1968). In the same way, the TV news every evening gives us the list of the day's sins and outrages, but it would not dare give us the longer list of the day's graces and goodness. Since, in media terms, goodness is not news.

Scripture scholar Wilfrid Harrington suggests that Jesus spoke these two parables in response to the needs of his own disciples. He was encouraging them to continue to sow the seed of the kingdom in spite of the "hindrance and apathy" that they were encountering, and he was responding, perhaps, to their lack of confidence in their own seemingly very small selves.

You and I may feel at times as the disciples of Jesus felt. Evil out there in the world is so widespread that it forces us to doubt that we can, realistically speaking, do anything worthwhile about it. And sin in here, in our hearts, still holds an attraction for us so that we feel ourselves unworthy to be the instruments by which Jesus spreads his kingdom over the earth in our time.

Yet we must continue to promote the kingdom in society even as we continue to work on improving ourselves. We must continue to believe that selflessness in the service of others will, at the same time, undermine the selfishness in ourselves. We must tell ourselves that Jesus did not choose perfect people when he chose the apostles as his co-workers in the work of the kingdom, and he has not done so in choosing us. Yet the Lord knows what he is doing!

Sometimes it may seem to us that the whole world is in the grip of the tyrants and the thugs, the bombers and the terrorists; that our streets are no more than conveyor belts for the drug barons; that honor has fled our various civic leaderships; that blind con-sumerism is consuming our soul; that our traditional national traits of hospitality and plain decency are folding their tents even in our smallest communities. And yet, for all of that, Jesus says that the kingdom of God is among us, and that it is growing imperceptibly day and night, and that it will expand. There is the sense of inevitable triumph in what Jesus says about God's reign, for the kingdom is the eternal plan and gift of God, and it is a matter of destiny!

We should read today's parables, then, as a summons to hope. They are a rejection of any talk of despair. They are a summoning of us to a renewal of our commitment to Christ's reign over our hearts, and to an increase of energy in our task of building the kingdom of God on the earth, in our communities, in our parishes, and in our families.

# 95B Twelfth Sunday in Ordinary Time

## MARK 4:35–41

### A Stormy Passage

Mark, in his Gospel, shows our Lord's disciples very much as reflections of our fragile selves, according to Wilfrid Harrington. Often the disciples are hesitant with regard to Jesus and fearful with regard to life. For these disciples, "life in the here and now is real and earnest and can be grim" *(New Testament Message: Mark)*. We see these facets of their characters and of life in today's Gospel scene.

Jesus has been preaching all day to the crowds on one side of the Sea of Galilee. When evening comes he says to his disciples, "Let us cross to the other side." As they cross over the sea, a violent storm blows up. The boat takes on water, and it is in danger of sinking. The disciples are terrified. Jesus sleeps through the storm on a cushion in the stern of the boat.

It must have been an unusual storm for the disciples to be terrified. Many of them were fishermen by trade and had lived their lives on this same sea. They had endured its storms and squalls a hundred times before. But now fear and panic grip them. You can sense it in the anguished way they shout at Jesus—almost accusingly— "Teacher, do you not care that we are perishing?"

Our Lord awakens and says to the sea, "Quiet! Be still!" These are the same words that Jesus spoke in the Gospel for the fourth Sunday in Ordinary Time when he expelled the demon from the possessed man. Scripture scholar William Barclay notes that the people of our Lord's time believed that the destructive forces of nature were as much the work of the demons as the destructive element in a possessed man.

The wind retreats and the sea calms in response to the command of Jesus. Then he turns to the disciples and says, "Why are you terrified? Do you not yet have faith?"

What are we to learn from these words and from this scene? The immediate lesson—in Mark's view—is for the Church in general. It's a lesson of encouragement for the Church of our time as it was for the Church of Mark's time. The lesson is that the Lord does not abandon his Church when it has confident faith in him. Bible scholar Wilfrid Harrington writes that the Church "may seem to be at the mercy of the forces pitted against it," but nothing will greatly harm it if it keeps faith with its Lord and in his continuing presence (*Mark: New Testament Message—A Biblical-Theological Commentary,* Collegeville, MN: Michael Glazier, 1979).

Deriving from this is a lesson for our parishes as well as for ourselves as individual believers. Jesus remains present with us all through life, and as much in its stormy passages as in its moments of calm. I think we are to learn that no threat or trial can overcome us as long as we retain trust and confidence in Christ. After all, he is committed to us and he proved it on the cross.

The English poet Robert Browning wrote, "We mortals cross the ocean of this world. Each in his average cabin of a life" ("Bishop Blougram's Apology"). The ocean of this world is both external and internal to us. We have many fears about the "out there" of life, and we have many anxieties about the "in here" of life. Our passage through this ocean of the outside and of the inside is steered from the small cabin or wheelhouse of myself. It is a very average wheelhouse indeed. And well we know it! I suspect that the Irish monk Saint Brendan the Navigator knew it too. I suspect that he was as aware of the turbulent psychological world inside himself as of the tempestuous world outside when he composed his lovely and deeply realistic prayer. We should make it our own: "Help me, O God, for my boat is so small and your sea is so great!"

A disciple is a learner. The disciples in today's Gospel are learners. Their panic in the storm and their lack of trust in the Lord tell us that they are still only beginners in the business of Christian discipleship. What shall we say of ourselves? Unlike these early disciples, many of us have been with the Lord for almost a lifetime. Have we progressed beyond the disciples in today's Gospel incident? We can answer for ourselves by looking back at the anxious moments and the panic passages of our lives.

We should have little trouble remembering how steady or how unsure was our trust in that Lord who never fails the disciple who has confidence in him.

# 98b Thirteenth Sunday in Ordinary Time

## MARK 5:21–43

### A Response to Faith

A solemn if psychologically fragile experience for the altar server of my childhood was the chanting of the *Dies irae* by the priests at the funeral Mass. Another soul from the parish had left us and gone off into the heavens to face his account with God.

The priest in the black vestments sent the soul on its way with the awesome gravity of the pre–Vatican II funeral ritual. *Dies irae! Dies illae!* the priests chanted in their powerful country voices. "Day of wrath, O that day!" they boomed—off-key!—in the strong, simple faith of that time. Somber strophe after somber strophe rolled down the aisle of the church like a river in winter flood, and bounced off the back wall and rose to fill the empty space of the church loft. It was providential that we didn't really know what the Latin lines meant, for the sepulchral voices and the steamrollering strophes frightened our tenderness and impressed us with the near hopeless condition of the late departed soul. And this, of course, was the condition that one day would be our very own!

The theological texture of those days, as reflected in the funeral liturgy, could hardly be more different from the theological texture of today. The Church has moved the funeral rite out of its former anxiety and into the sure hope of the Resurrection. It has replaced apprehension with celebration. What prevailed in funeral theology, when I was an altar boy, was partly a hand-me-down from Judaism. We see some of this Jewish theology and funeral customs at work in the Gospel scene of today's Mass. And we see, by way of contrast, the thinking of Jesus with regard to them. The "commotion" that offended Jesus as he approached the house where the dead daughter of Jairus lay was mostly the loud weeping and wailing that was part of Jewish funerals. Some of this wailing and crying was genuine and heartfelt, but much of it was professionally staged. Hired flute players orchestrated the mourning for the girl. Hair was torn from the head to signal the mind distraught over so huge a loss. Garments were rent to express the rending of the heart within. All water jars in the house were emptied because the angel of death had entered the house and contaminated it. The water would be replaced after the funeral, much as we empty our holy water fonts for the period that Christ lies in the tomb and refill them later with the Easter water of new life. Joy was forbidden: grief was mandatory.

Contrasted with this tumult is the serenity of Jesus, and his ability to bring hope and life into the human quandary. Contrasted, too, is the steady faith of Jairus in Jesus and the distracted funeral liturgy that is already in full swing at the behest of those members of the family who, unlike Jairus, had no faith in Jesus. We see in today's Gospel what we've seen in the other Gospel incidents of the past few Sundays (the storm-tossed sea, the man convulsed, the ostracized leper, the paralytic lowered through the roof): we see that whereas people panic or lose hope, Jesus never does. He is the one who comes along with the practical solution, with the compassion that is effective, and with the sympathy that gives life.

So let us trust this Jesus. We have every reason from the Gospels to do so. Never let go of him. He will see you through the rough times and the dark passages and the days of great loss. He will give you the form of healing he knows is best suited to your need. And he will be there to take your hand on that day we used to call the *Dies irae,* the day of wrath. It is no longer a day to be dreaded with our hand in his.

# 101B Fourteenth Sunday in Ordinary Time

## MARK 6:1–6

### The Closed Heart

This episode involving Jesus and the people of "his native place" (namely, Nazareth and its surroundings) has deep meaning for our Gospel writer Mark. According to Bible scholar Wilfrid Harrington (*Mark: New Testament Message—A Biblical-Theological Commentary,* Collegeville, MN: Michael Glazier, 1979), Mark finds in this episode that while Jesus is accepted by "outsiders" he is rejected by "his own." Mark found that he himself was experiencing the same pastoral problem in the early days of the Church.

The Gentiles, generally speaking, were accepting the Gospel of Jesus; the Jewish people were not. Perhaps Mark also found a measure of consolation when comparing his own pastoral impasse with that experienced by the Lord in "his native place."

At any rate, when Jesus comes into his home territory he is confronted with the closed heart. He finds the closed heart among those who know him best and who ought to be the ones most proud of him. For he is, so to speak, the local boy who has made good. His name is known throughout the land of Israel and even beyond its borders. So, in consequence, is the name of the place he comes from. He is known widely as Jesus of Nazareth, or the Nazarene. In this way, he has brought great honor to Nazareth and to the people among whom he grew up.

But, what happens? He runs up against a brick wall right here at home. The people react incredulously to him. They question the source of his knowledge and of his wisdom. They question the source of his works of healing and of cleansing. Now since the source cannot be his family ("Is he not the carpenter, the son of Mary? . . . Are not his sisters here with us?" they say disparagingly), they may be concluding, as the scribes had said earlier, that Satan is the source. While the people have asked the right questions with regard to Jesus and his great gifts, they nevertheless come to the entirely wrong conclusion! Wilfrid Harrington notes: "They cannot bring themselves to believe in the greatness or in the mission of a man who is one of themselves" (*Mark: New Testament Message A Biblical-Theological Commentary*, Collegeville, MN: Michael Glazier, 1979).

There is a terribly abrupt ending to what should have been a joyous homecoming scene. It is terribly abrupt both from the people's point of view and from the Lord's point of view. The Gospel says simply, "And they took offense at him." Our Lord is shocked at this. It is a wholly unexpected reaction on the part of his own people! That they find him too much for them is not the result of their mind's analysis but of their closed heart. Resentment permeates the lines of this Gospel episode. The people among whom Jesus grew up resent his success in a manner that can only be described as irrational.

And they resent Jesus' family—their very neighbors—their blessedness. Jesus, a local boy, has become too successful! Why should his family be so singularly blessed by God in preference to the other families of the same faith and station? The people close their hearts to Jesus and to his family. No wonder he is shocked! No wonder he is so distressed by their lack of faith in him that he is not able to work any miracle of consequence among them. To use contemporary idiom, he cannot function in this hostile climate; he cannot penetrate such massed and negative psychology.

None of us, I imagine, has ever been in quite the kind of situation that Jesus found himself in. We haven't come up against the depth of resentment that fuelled the disbelief and even the offense that faced Jesus in today's Gospel incident. But we do appreciate how instinctively we are tempted to resent the successes of those we know well. And we appreciate how easily our resentfulness clouds our better judgment and closes our heart.

Let us guard against resentment and closed-heartedness. Let us not resent people their good fortune or success or, above all, their God-given calling and blessedness. And less us not belittle anyone of different color, ethnic origin, creed, or social condition. The most gifted on the one hand, and the least fortunate on the other hand, are always the people that don't fit the closed heart.

Jesus marveled when he found resentment and blockage where he least expected them, in his native place and among his own people. We, who follow him, should marvel too when we find resentment and blockage in fellow Christians and in our own hearts.

# 104B Fifteenth Sunday in Ordinary Time

## MARK 6:7–13

### The Call to Repentance

We cannot go through life without our dreams. Our dreams are the goals and the ideals we have for ourselves and for the world as we would like it to be. Call these dreams our hopes, our desires, our longings. Martin Luther King Jr. famously said, "I have a dream." He meant, of course, a vision of America at its integrated best.

T. E. Lawrence, in *Seven Pillars of Wisdom* (New York: Penguin, 1976), writes, "All men dream, but not equally. Those who dream by night in the dusty recesses of their minds wake in the day to find that it was vanity. But the dreamers of the day are dangerous men, for they may act their dream with open eyes, to make it possible."

Now Jesus was a dreamer of the day. The dream he had was the greatest dream anyone ever dreamed. It was the dream of men and women turning their backs on sin and entering the kingdom of God; the dream of people living their lives as life was lived by our Blessed Lord. In today's Gospel, Jesus sends out the apostles to preach repentance as the altogether necessary first step.

He sends them out two by two. This was the traditional Jewish arrangement. Each apostle takes a single walking stick. The stick or staff was also traditional, and it eased the long journey and warded-off the dangers of the road and of the night. The apostles do not take seconds of anything with them; they do not take replacements. They must travel light for they are men on a mission. When they enter a place and find a hospitable house, they are to stay there for the duration of their preaching and not search for a better lodging. The scholars tell us that all of these details are meant to reflect the urgency of the mission of preaching repentance as preface to entering the kingdom of God. These details also teach the apostles to place their trust in the providence of God.

If a community refuses to listen to them, they are to leave that community and, as they exit its boundary, to shake the dust of its streets off their feet as a mark of disgust at the community's lack of faith. No doubt such an action might make the community reconsider its rejection of the apostles' message, for they are Jews, and to shake the dust of your sandals at people is the same as calling them heathens and their community unclean.

The quality of our own repentance may be evaluated in the light of today's Gospel. First of all, repentance is the necessary preface to membership in the kingdom of God. It is deep and it is heartfelt. Today's Gospel will not allow us any way around deep and heartfelt repentance. Some of us, for any number of reasons, may have slipped back into the ways of the world. And, at the moment, we may be wishing things were right again in our lives but we are avoiding heartfelt repentance and trying to settle for what is compromisingly and clearly less than the kingdom requirement. We may be doing this only because we don't appreciate the weight of the scripture's words in the matter of heartfelt repentance.

And if we are pastors and preachers, we may be comparatively silent about the call to heartfelt repentance because we are genuinely afraid to "push the envelope" of the fragile faith of our time. While all of this is understandable, it neglects the integrity of today's Gospel message in which repentance is an entirely necessary change of heart in anyone who wishes to be part of the kingdom. Repentance is not a kingdom option: it is a kingdom fundamental.

Repentance, of its very nature, hurts the heart and upsets one's lifestyle. It is meant to. Bible scholar William Barclay says: "It is bound to hurt, for it involves the bitter realization that the way we were following is wrong. It is bound to disturb, because it means a complete reversal of life" (*The Gospel of Mark: The New Daily Study Bible,* Nashville, TN: Westminster John Knox Press, 2001). But repentance has its positive side too. It introduces us to a lifetime of inner peace and joy, and to delight in God's word and direction. That, I sense, is the gift which is being denied some of us in this generation when we are not called—or when we do not call ourselves—vigorously to repentance.

# 107B Sixteenth Sunday in Ordinary Time

## MARK 6:30–34

### Compassion and Care

All of us can identify with this scene. Jesus and the apostles are exhausted from preaching and teaching and healing the throngs that follow them. They need to rest and to recharge their spiritual batteries. We feel the same way ourselves at times. We need to get away from it all. We need a little space just to be alone with God.

But our children keep us at their beck and call, and our parishioners rely on our continual availability. Modern life is so full of work and meetings and schedules! I knew an exceptionally busy pastor whose parishioners described him as a revolving door. Such, apparently, have been Jesus and the apostles up to this moment. So the Lord says to them in today's Gospel, "Come away by yourselves to a deserted place and rest a little."

But what happens? As soon as the throngs see them leave in the boat for the far side of the lake, they race around the curve of the shore so that they are there to meet Jesus when the boat pulls in! If this happened to us we might throw up our hands in exasperation— or in anger. We might feel that our scant privacy is being invaded by a thoughtless and self-centered mob. But what does Jesus do? The Bible says, ". . . his heart was moved with pity for them, for they were like sheep without a shepherd; and he began to teach them many things." He rolled up his sleeves, so to speak, and taught them at length and attended to their needs as if he were already fully rested and refreshed.

That line, "His heart was moved with pity for them, for they were like sheep without a shepherd," must catch our eye. It needs to be underlined in our hearts because, from among all the facts that we know about Jewish shepherds and their sheep, nothing was more central and pastoral than the dedication of the Jewish shepherd to his sheep, and their following of him exclusively as their unique shepherd. They would follow no one else. Our Lord is the Good Shepherd, and he knows in his heart of hearts that these people have chosen him as their exclusive shepherd. They have left their scribes and their rabbis— their theologians and pastors—to attach themselves to him. His compassion will not allow him to do other than attend to their needs even though it costs him his sparse privacy and his necessary rest.

Bible scholar William Barclay writes, "A sheep without its shepherd simply cannot find its pasture" (*The Gospel of Mark: The New Daily Study Bible*, Nashville, TN: Westminster John Knox Press, 2001). A number of years ago, I was assigned to an inner-city parish. I occasionally would walk on a weekend night through the streets of the town near the parish rectory. The streets were full of night clubs and bars, and fast-food restaurants, tourists, and college students. I saw some things indeed! Some of those I met were out of it on drugs and drink. Some of them were disconnected from their families and from their homes.

Some might still have gone to Sunday Mass if they were sober, but sobriety did not seem to be a feature of their weekend lives. Were these people the contemporary images of this Gospel reading's "sheep without a shepherd"?

Those of us who are responsible for others, especially parents and pastors, may not realize how important we are in our children's lives and in our parishioners' lives, and how much they depend on us for nurturing and shepherding. It is no exaggeration to say that parent and pastor are pivotal in the lives of these others. We should not accept this fact only in terms of its calling of us to accountability but, more so, in terms of our divine election to the task. Our children and our parishioners, ignorant or doubting, are God's gift to us. And at the end of the day, when all the arguments for and against these modern spiritual nomads are in, they remain in God's eyes "my sheep . . . the sheep of my pasture" (Ezekiel 34:31).

# 110B Seventeenth Sunday in Ordinary Time

## JOHN 6:1–15

### Bread for the World

There was a time when religion was accused of diverting the poor's attention from their hunger—from their lack of bread and their lack of the bread of justice—by stressing the next life while playing down the importance of this one. In place of bread and justice, religion was said to promise the poor "a pie in the sky when you die."

This charge against religion was true to some extent, for various authorities in the past used religion to distract the masses from their plight—and from embarking upon revolution. Napoleon once famously said that religion kept the poor from murdering the rich.

But the Christian religion is not in the business of promoting the next life while ignoring present-life hunger and poverty. Religion is not about keeping one class going at the expense of the poorer classes. If we look with open eyes at the Gospel we find our Lord fighting hunger and poverty, sickness and disease as often and as devotedly as he fights Satan and sin. Why is this?

Jesus did not fight poverty and disease because he was a humanitarian and wished to establish a purely secular utopia on earth. He fought hunger and poverty and sickness and disease because the scripture links them with sin. They enter history with original sin and as its consequence. And they are reflections of continuing sin on the earth. Sin, indeed, causes all forms of human bondage. Every form of bondage lessens our humanity. Every form of bondage lessens the image of God in us.

And so, through today's Gospel, you and I are being taught that the next life is not unrelated to present life, and that glory in heaven follows on our commitment to restoring this earth in Christ. Religion, then, serves both worlds. The Christian ministry is a ministry that serves the full range of human need in this life even as it prepares human beings for the next. The ministry serves the body as well as the soul.

The great crowd that follows Jesus in today's Gospel scene becomes hungry. Like all the hungry faces that we see on our TV screens from Africa to Afghanistan, they do not complain very much. Hunger has a way of silencing people. The great lords of the earth have always known this, and they have used it to their advantage to keep the poor in line. Our Lord notices the crowd's hunger too. But he notices it compassionately. And he will alleviate it. The people have not brought food with them in their haste to follow Jesus, to hear him and to be near him. There is very little bread among them: only five barley loaves, according to Andrew. Yet from those five loaves Jesus creates sufficient bread to feed everyone until they are full. And there are twelve baskets of fragments left over.

There are several lessons for us in this feeding scene. The first, of course, is the compassion of Christ and, consequently, our own call as Christians to be compassionate. The second lesson is the binding together of religion and human need, liturgy and life. Our God is an immanent God; i.e., a hands-on God, in this Gospel scene. The Christian must be a hands-on believer, not a "pie in the sky when you die" one. A third lesson is the range of our Lord's ministry and, therefore, the range of our own. It is a ministry to the whole person. Our Lord feeds the soul with his word and grace and the body with its necessary bread. A fourth lesson is the abundance of Christ's compassion and love as a challenge to the depth of our own com-passion and love. The abundance is signed by the twelve basketsful left over. A fifth lesson may be the foreshadowing of the Eucharist as humanity's ultimate bread, for Catholic commentators see, in the rubric of blessing that Jesus used before multiplying the boy's bread, a prefiguring of the Eucharist to come.

Over the next few Sundays, the Gospel will deal with other aspects of the relationship between Jesus and bread. It will deal with bread in its several spiritual, and in its singular eucharistic senses.

But for today, we stay with our Lord's multiplication of the loaves of ordinary bread to feed the hungry crowd. Let us thank God for our daily bread, for the ordinary bread that Jesus made available to the hungry crowd in today's Gospel and the food he puts on our own tables at home every day. Let us accept the challenge of connecting liturgy with life, of connecting the next world with this one, of seeing hunger and poverty as social sin, and of opposing them with an abundance of active compassion.

Meanwhile, I commend you for your marvelous support of the special collections and Catholic relief agencies that help to put food in the mouths of a third of the world. You are a truly outstanding parish in this regard. I do not believe that we are far from God with the hungry and the poor of the earth always on our hearts and in our pockets.

# 113b Eighteenth Sunday in Ordinary Time

## John 6:24–35

### The Bread of Truth

The sixth chapter of John's Gospel is a long chapter. It began last Sunday with the lovely story of Jesus multiplying the five barley loaves and feeding the hungry crowd. Jesus refers to that feeding scene when he says to the crowd in today's Gospel, "You are looking for me not because you saw signs [indicators of Jesus' messiahship] but because you ate the loaves and were filled."

Today, Jesus begins what the commentators call his discourse on bread. He discusses several forms of bread with the crowd (including his disciples). Some of these forms have appeared already in history such as "our daily bread" and the "manna from heaven." These are bread in the ordinary sense of the word, food which sustains the body. Another form of bread that has appeared in Jewish history is a spiritual form of bread. It is the word of God spoken by the prophets. Jesus, in today's Gospel and over the next few Sundays, will discuss these and other kinds of bread with the crowd. This is his "discourse on bread."

We met the first form of bread in last Sunday's Gospel. Jesus fed the hungry crowd with the bread multiplied from the five barley loaves. This was ordinary bread. It is the same bread we pray for in the Our Father. Jesus was very pleased to feed it to those who were hungry. Today, however, he feels that he must caution the crowd, for they are tempted to follow him only because he feeds their stomachs. He tells them that they must be more concerned about a very different kind of bread. He calls it "the bread of God which comes down from heaven and gives life to the world."

What is this bread? It is Jesus himself. It is the saving word he speaks. It is the truth of God he speaks. Why is Jesus the truth of God? In today's Gospel Jesus says that God the Father "has set his seal" on him. This means that God guarantees the truth of which Jesus speaks. If you find a seal on a shipment of goods, you are looking at the shipper's guarantee that all is in order. If you find a seal on your school diploma, you are looking at the school's guarantee that you completed the course of studies successfully. Now God's seal is on Jesus. God guarantees that Jesus speaks his truth.

Scripture scholar William Barclay tells us that the rabbis had a saying: "The seal of God is truth." Barclay further tells us that the Jewish Talmud has this story. One day all the experts in the Law were gathered in assembly. A little scroll fell from heaven among them. When they opened it they found only one word written. It was the word *truth*. In Hebrew, the word *truth* is made up of the first, middle, and last letters of the alphabet. Truth, comments the Talmud, is the seal of God. Now, if the seal of God is on Jesus—and it is—then Jesus is the truth of God. And he is the whole truth of God—the beginning, the middle, and the end of it. Jesus is, then, the bread of truth which is more important than ordinary bread.

Thoughtful people search for the truth today. Thoughtful people always have. And thoughtful people always will. More than anything else, thoughtful people search for one particular kind of truth—saving truth. Saving truth gives ground zero meaning to our lives now, destroys death, and will take us beyond the confines of the grave. Jesus says, in today's Gospel, that he is this saving truth, the truth that "endures for eternal life."

What our Lord said to the people two thousand years ago he is still saying to the searchers of truth in this generation. He is saying, "Follow me because I am God's truth and his seal is on me." He is saying, "Follow me because I am the truth that saves, and the truth that gives ground zero meaning to your present life, and the truth that guarantees you a future beyond death." Jesus is the truth that "gives life to the world"—the bread that "endures for eternal life."

I want us to cherish these guarantees of Christ to us who follow him. I want the bread of his words to calm our hearts in the rough patches of life, and to fortify our hope of glory. I want us to keep on challenging our young people and our lapsed friends with Jesus as the bread of life, the only truth that matters, and the One on whom God has set his seal. He so merits their attention and, ultimately, their love.

I saw a bumper sticker one time which read, "Wise Men Still Seek Him." I want us to pray, in response to our Lord's words in today's Gospel, that all the lonely people out there, caught in the ambushes of life, will be given the grace to seek Jesus, and the grace to find him. For he is the bread of truth without which the years of our lives are not much more than the years of a famished existence.

# 116B Nineteenth Sunday in Ordinary Time

## JOHN 6:41–51

### The Bread from Heaven

Jesus calls himself the bread that came down from heaven. Why does our Lord call himself bread? I suppose it's because of the fact that the people listening to him used bread as their primary food. Bread is the staff of life. It is essential to our existence. We die without it. We develop healthfully with it. The people listening to Jesus would have had no trouble in appreciating the central importance of bread.

They also appreciated how crucial to their ancestors was the manna that fell from heaven. Their ancestors spent 40 years on the Exodus from Egypt to the Promised Land. One time, during that journey, they had nothing left to eat. God answered their plight by sending them manna. They called it the bread from heaven. It fell around their camps during the night, and they collected it fresh each morning (see Exodus 16).

Our Lord, tapping into this sacred Jewish memory, tells the people that he is bread from heaven in a far superior form to the manna their ancestors were given. For the ancestors ate but died eventually nonetheless; whereas anyone who eats the living bread that is Jesus "will live forever."

Jesus, I suspect, is giving in today's Gospel the interpretation of the words that he spoke at an earlier time when he said, "One does not live by bread alone, but by every word that comes forth from the mouth of God" (Matthew 4:4). The words that proceed from the mouth of God are as necessary to the life of the soul as is ordinary bread to the life of the body.

God has spoken many words over the many generations. They are all bread from heaven to feed our souls. Those spoken words are the Ten Commandments. Those words are also the words of the prophets, spoken sometimes as chastisement, sometimes as challenge, sometimes as comfort, but always as spiritual nourishment for the soul. Now, if men and women live by every word that has ever come forth from the mouth of God, all the more completely do they live when nourished with Jesus, "the living bread that came down from heaven."

The letter to the Hebrews begins with this statement: "In times past, God spoke in partial and various ways to our ancestors through the prophets; in these last days, he spoke to us through a son whom he made heir of all things and through whom he created the universe" (Hebrews 1:1–2). Jesus is not another "partial" word of God. He is the full word of God. And he is the definitive word of God. And he is the final word of God. He is absolutely everything we need for a healthful spiritual life and for holiness. He so fashions us in unity with himself that we will ascend to glory, as he did, at the end of our lives on earth.

The reaction of the crowd to Jesus' claim to be the living bread that has come down from heaven is to start questioning his pedigree. They say, "Is this not Jesus, the son of Joseph? Do we not know his father and mother? Then how can he say, 'I have come down from heaven'?" There is irony here. The people who react in this way to Jesus' self-definition as the living bread come down from heaven are the very same people whom Jesus fed with the miraculous multiplication of the loaves just a short while before. Are they being honest in rejecting his words now when they so eagerly accepted and applauded his marvelous feeding miracle then?

And what of honesty in the present generation? There are people today who pick and choose among the teachings of Jesus. There are some who use the Church when it suits them. There are others whose commitment to Christ hinges on the caliber of their Bishop and priest rather than on the quality of their personal relationship with Jesus.

There are people who use others' sins and scandals as excuses for their own lack of accountability before the Lord. Do they honestly think that God cannot see through these tactics and blocking mechanisms? Are these people the modern counterparts of those whom John says "murmured about [Jesus]" and whom we find in our Lord's face in today's Gospel reading?

It is for them to answer. You and I accept the faith for what it really is: the obedient and graceful following of Christ and not the following of excuses. With all our hearts we accept him as our spiritual "bread of life, . . . the living bread that came down from heaven."

# 119B Twentieth Sunday in Ordinary Time

## JOHN 6:51–58

### The Eucharistic Bread

You will recall that Jesus, in the Gospel readings of the past two Sundays, has been speaking of himself as the bread of life in the present tense. He has been saying, "I am the bread of life" and "I am the living bread that came down from heaven." You may notice that in the first line of today's Gospel he switches to the future tense. He speaks of a new kind of bread, future bread. He calls it "the bread that I will give." A few lines later, he names this bread his "flesh" and "blood."

In what sense does Jesus give us his flesh and blood? To a Jew of our Lord's time, "flesh and blood" represented the whole person. We can say that Jesus gave himself wholly in several ways. First, he gave himself wholly in his complete obedience to his Father's will. Then he gave himself wholly on the cross for us. And just before he did so, he gave himself wholly ("flesh and blood") to the disciples at the Last Supper, under the appearances of bread and wine.

Here in today's Gospel, even though the Last Supper is still in the future, John reflects our eucharistic understanding of Jesus' words. In fact, throughout John's recording of the Lord's entire discussion with the crowd on the subject of bread, the Eucharist is never far from John's mind; and there are what scripture scholar James McPolin calls "indirect reminders" of it in such phrases as "bread of life" and "living bread" (*John: New Testament Message*, Vol. 6, Collegeville, MN: Michael Glazier, 1979).

Jesus says, "Whoever eats my flesh and drinks my blood has eternal life, and I will raise him on the last day." You and I understand these words in line with the Church's traditional understanding of them. We understand them as the Eucharist. We accept the Lord's words in faith. The Eucharist is a mystery of faith. But if it is a mystery of faith, it is also a mystery of divine love. And it is a mystery of divine presence. The Eucharist is Christ himself, "body and blood, soul and divinity . . . and, therefore, the whole Christ . . . truly, really, and substantially contained" (*Catechism of the Catholic Church,* [CCC], 1374). It is the flesh and blood of Christ, and as the Bible scholar Neal M. Flanagan writes, it is his flesh and blood "as the Spirit-filled flesh and blood of the heavenly Son of Man" (*The Gospel According to John and the Johannine Epistles, Collegeville Bible Commentary,* Vol. 4, Collegeville, MN: Liturgical Press, 1983).

May we take a few moments now to refresh our minds and hearts on three components of the Eucharist? These are: the Eucharist as sacrifice, as communion, and as presence. As sacrifice, the Eucharist re-enacts and re-presents the sacrificial death of Jesus. Christ's saving passover is remembered in the Eucharist, and it is made present. In this manner, we are able to offer the Father our greatest form of worship—the gift most pleasing to him, his beloved Son. In return, the fruits of Christ's sacrifice are made available to us.

As spiritual food and communion, the Eucharist unites us in a singular way with Jesus. That singular way is contained in his words, "Whoever eats my flesh and drinks my blood remains in me and I in him. Just as the living Father sent me and I have life because of the Father, so also the one who feeds on me will have life because of me" (John 6:56–57). In addition, the Eucharist "preserves, increases and renews the life of grace [which we] received at Baptism," and it separates us from sin and increases our charity (CCC, 1392).

The Eucharist is, also, the most complete form of Christ's presence available to us this side of glory. I encourage you, then, to visit the Lord in the tabernacle with your cares and troubles, and your love and devotion. You will find rest there. And peace for your soul. And encouragement and inspiration too.

The Eucharist, whether as sacrifice, heavenly food, or divine presence, is a marvel of God's love for us. It is a marvel of union, for all true love is ultimately a matter of union. The Eucharist is Christ's union with us and our engrafting to him. It is the coming into being of the deepest love and union he has always sought with us, that deepest love and union which he pointed forward to in the image of the branch adhering to the vine (cf. John 15:1–10). As scripture scholar Eugene Boylan writes, "Our Lord instituted the blessed Eucharist so that we might become one entity with himself, united to him as the head is united to the body, and as food is united to one that consumes it" (*This Tremendous Lover,* Notre Dame, IN: Ave Maria Press, 1987).

If, as scripture scholar Michael Mullins writes, "the gift of manna was seen by the Jews as the greatest of Moses' miracles" (*The Gospel of John,* Co. Dublin: Columba Press, 2004), may we, in our turn, see the Eucharist as the greatest of the Lord's gifts to us on our journey through life to the heavenly homeland.

# 122B Twenty-first Sunday in Ordinary Time

## JOHN 6:60–69

### Accepting Jesus through the Spirit

With today's Gospel, Jesus comes to the end of his theology of bread. He has led his hearers through the different ways in which he is the bread of God. He is the living bread come down from heaven: the bread of saving truth and the bread of moral truth. He is the bread that satisfies the hunger of the heart. And he is the superior manna, the eucharistic bread, that feeds us on our pilgrim way and pledges eternal life.

Over the past few Sunday Gospels, our Lord has been making these statements as part of an overall, or major, statement as to who he really is. He is, in fact, the very wisdom of God in the flesh. In consequence, he has been making a major faith demand of those who have been listening to him, and of those who would follow him in future ages, including ourselves. He is no passing manna from heaven, but the living bread of God come down from heaven. He is no new prophet or holy man with a "partial" word of God (cf. Hebrews 1:1), but the full wisdom of God incarnate.

Those who listen to the Lord murmur and contest his words among themselves. Jesus seems to stretch the demand of faith further, for them and for us, when he says, "What if you were to see the Son of Man ascending to where he was before?" He is intimating his ascension into glory.

Our Lord's great statement as to who he really is, his self-definition, in this sixth chapter of Saint John's Gospel requires both a deep faith and a high moral life in those who would accept him as the wisdom of God. I do not think that we are capable of this deep faith and of this high moral life if we depend on our own unaided selves. Quite simply, we have to depend on the Holy Spirit.

Jesus says, "It is the spirit that gives life, while the flesh is of no avail." To be a Christian, and a eucharistic Christian, calls for deep faith. But faith has weakened all around us today. Society is heavily secularized and there is considerable religious indifference.

The wisdom of God, incarnate in Jesus, is not allowed to impact sufficiently our social problems or even our personal problems. The so-called Christian West, while respectful of Jesus, is also largely ignorant of him and uncommitted to his vision and his values. The British poet Rev. G. A. Studdert Kennedy writes of the multitudes who are indifferent to Jesus (and to the poor who are the face of Jesus) as they hustle and bustle through their lives. They are neither with Christ nor against him. They simply "pass him by" ("Indifference," *The Unutterable Beauty*). May we, at least, as individual Catholics and as this parish community, be saved from indifference and from the situation in which religion is mainly a coloration in our lives but never quite a commitment.

In last Sunday's Gospel, Jesus turned to the Twelve and asked, "Do you also want to leave me?" Would they leave him because he declared himself to be the key to salvation? Would they leave him because of his challenging words on the Eucharist? Would they leave him because following him required a deep faith and commitment to the highest of moral standards? Would they leave him because he claimed to be the wisdom of God incarnate? In their time, the Twelve were given the grace, by the Holy Spirit, to see that Jesus' words are not things of flesh but, as Jesus says in today's Gospel, "words of spirit and life." And so they were empowered by the Holy Spirit to answer Jesus through Peter, "Master, to whom shall we go? You have the words of eternal life."

In this generation, you and I are among those who have been given the grace, through the Holy Spirit, to answer Jesus as Peter answered him. We accept that Jesus' words are not words of the flesh and not words of the world. They are, as he said, the words of spirit and life. We have been given the greatest of graces: the grace to follow Jesus and his way of doing things because we have been empowered to acknowledge him as the wisdom of God incarnate. This is not the mark of our own doing, but the mark of God's mysterious favor toward us.

# 125 B Twenty-second Sunday in Ordinary Time

## Mark 7:1–8, 14–15, 21–23

### Getting in God's Way

This incident involving Jesus and the Pharisees and the experts in the Law is critical to the Lord's understanding of religion, and to our own understanding of religion.

At first sight, the incident is over a small matter. It is an argument about washing hands—and pots and cups and dinner dishes. The Pharisees and the legal experts challenge Jesus over the behavior of some of his disciples. These disciples do not observe the prescribed ritual washings and so do "not follow the traditions of the elders." What were these "traditions of the elders"? The main tradition to be followed was, of course, the Law of God. The Law of God meant the Ten Commandments and the Pentateuch, or first five books of the Bible. These books contain moral principles and regulations. The interpretation of these principles and regulations was—rightly— a matter of great pastoral concern to the Jewish people. But it gave rise eventually to the scribes, or the experts in the Law, and this is where the difficulty arose. This is where men's rules got in God's way.

These men had what Barclay calls "a passion for definition" and, over the centuries, they broke down the Law into thousands of little rules and regulations governing every aspect of Jewish life. These thousands of rules were not written down in a book. They were passed down orally through the generations and were known as the Oral Law. It is this Oral Law—"the traditions of the elders"—that some of Jesus' disciples were not following. In the eyes of the Pharisees and the scribes, the disciples are guilty of transgressing the Oral Law—and so is Jesus because he allowed them to do so.

The Oral Law was greatly concerned with ritual purity. The ceremonial washing of one's hands, for example, was an exact and detailed matter. Before one even began the washing rite, the finger nails had to be free of dirt and dust. It is little wonder then that some categories of persons, such as the mentally disturbed, the lepers, and the shepherds, were not in a position to fulfill these requirements and were considered to be ritually unclean. A woman after childbirth was also considered to be unclean until she was ritually cleansed. Bible scholar Wilfrid Harrington notes, that "the principle of clean and unclean was at the root of Jewish preoccupation with ritual purification" (*Mark: New Testament Message—A Biblical-Theological Commentary,* Collegeville, MN: Michael Glazier, 1979).

So dominating was this Oral Law that it could be said to mask the Law of God, however unintentionally. Jesus, in today's Gospel, rejects these man-made rules and ritual distinctions. He says, in effect, that religious cleanliness or uncleanness is not decided by external rules but is a matter of what is within a person. He says, "Nothing that enters one from outside can defile that person; but the things that come out from within are what defile." It is not external factors and ritual rules that decide our cleanliness before God but the condition of our hearts. It is persons, not things, who commit sin. The living of the authentic religious life is a matter of the heart. It is what is inside us and what comes out from inside us that determines whether we are clean or unclean in God's eyes.

Our Lord accuses the Pharisees and scribes of hypocrisy. They are so consumed by the externals of religion that they have lost its spirit. As all of us know, it is easy to lose the spirit of a project for concern over its precise implementation; to get lost in rules and regulations and red tape; to lose the spirit for the letter. The prophet

Isaiah faulted his generation for this same degeneration in their religion. He spoke for the Lord God when he said, "This people honors me with their lips; but their hearts are far from me; in vain do they worship me, teaching as doctrines human precepts" (Isaiah 29:13). Our Lord quotes these same words in his response to the Pharisees and the scribes in today's Gospel reading.

Jesus calls for heart in our religious observances, and for spirit as opposed to lip service. Biblical scholar William Barclay writes, "There is no greater religious peril than that of identifying religion with outward observance. There is no commoner religious mistake than to identify goodness with certain so-called religious acts. . . . The fundamental question is: How is one's heart towards God and towards others" (*The Gospel of Mark: The New Daily Study Bible*, Nashville, TN: Westminster John Knox Press, 2001).

# 128b Twenty-third Sunday in Ordinary Time

## Mark 7:31–37

### Doing Things Well

When the people said of Jesus, "He has done all things well!" they were echoing the book of Genesis (1:31) in relation to God's handiwork in the creation story. All that God wrought in the six days of creation was found to be "good" and even "very good." God did everything well!

When I was a child, my next door neighbor stood on top of a stable at the end of his backyard. "There are two ways of doing everything: the right way and the wrong way," he said as he put the finishing touches to a roof of perfectly aligned tiles. The roof would protect his prize pony through the long winter. Even as a child, and even though at that age I was more interested in the welfare of the pony than in the well-being of my neighbor, I knew the man had done his job well!

In today's Gospel story of the healing of the man who was both deaf and mute, we should look for the reasons why the people were so astonished at this healing that Jesus performed and why they concluded, "He has done all things well!" First of all, the miracle takes place in the district of the Decapolis or the Ten Cities. This was Phoenician territory and, hence, Gentile territory. In our Gospel reading last Sunday, Jesus "wiped out the distinction between clean and unclean foods" (Barclay).

In today's Gospel Jesus wipes out the distinction between Jew and Gentile. This was an amazing development to the Jewish theological mind. The location of this healing—in pagan territory—tells us that Gospel and grace are as available to Gentile as to Jew. In terms of salvation, the Gentiles can no longer be regarded as unclean people. This, surely, is one reason for the people's amazement. Here is a second reason. The people said, "He has done all things well." The allusion here is to God's work of creation in the book of Genesis. We may assume that the people saw in this healing miracle, and in the one which preceded it concerning the Syrophoenician woman's afflicted daughter, the undoing by Jesus of the sinfulness that was soiling God's wonderful work of creation. John the Baptist had called it "the sin of the world" (John 1:29). So the people said of Jesus what Genesis said of God: He has done all things well.

Third, a person deaf and mute was a person severely afflicted. Such a one could not hear the word of God or speak God's praises in the assembly. He was thus severely afflicted religiously as well as physically. But in our Gospel story, Jesus opens the man's ears and releases his tongue so he may function on both levels. There is an allusion here to the book of the prophet Isaiah when the people express their astonishment and say, "He makes the deaf hear and the mute speak!" (cf. Isaiah 35:5–6).

Isaiah spoke his words with reference to the age of the messiah. In effect, the people are intimating that the messianic age has arrived in the person of Jesus.

As always, dear friends, the Gospel stories are recorded not just for the purpose of storytelling but that you and I may be confident in the One in whom we have placed our trust for healing and for salvation. They are recorded not only to tell the story of Jesus, but to strengthen our faith and to elicit our response. May our response to this Gospel today be our commitment to doing all things well in our religious, family, social, business, and personal lives.

# 131B Twenty-fourth Sunday in Ordinary Time

## MARK 8:27–35

### Saying No to Self

Today's Gospel reading brings us two defining moments in the lives of Peter and the disciples. First, the disciples, through Peter, acknowledge Jesus as the Messiah.

Second, through our Lord's rebuke of Peter, they learn that the messiah must be a suffering messiah. In consequence, you and I learn the pastoral lesson that there is no authentic Christian living without our sharing in the cross of Christ. It was Saint Paul's boast that he bore on his body the marks of the crucified Christ (see Galatians 6:17).

In our Lord's time, a suffering messiah was foreign to everyone's expectation (Is it all that different today?). Everyone wanted a glorious messiah who would usher in a glorious era of peace and plenty, of grandeur and glory for Israel. Suffering was not a part of this expectation and, less so, the scandal of the cross. Our Lord's abrupt treatment of Peter—"Get behind me, Satan!"—serves to impress on Peter and on the disciples the central role of the cross in Christ's life, and hence in our own Christian lives as well.

Saint Mark, writes Bible scholar Wilfrid Harrington, had to face the same issue with his contemporaries as Jesus had to face with Peter. "The confession of Peter is the facile profession of too many of Mark's contemporaries: You are the Christ. But everything depends on what they mean by that profession and its influence on their lives. They cannot have a risen Lord without a suffering messiah. They cannot be his disciples without walking his road of suffering" (*Mark:*

*New Testament Message—A Biblical-Theological Commentary,*
Collegeville, MN: Michael Glazier, 1979). It would seem that many
of Mark's contemporaries, as Peter and the disciples previously,
wished to walk with a Christ without his cross.

So today, as in Mark's time, there are many who want a
glorious Christ but not a pained and suffering one. They want a happy
religion but not a disciplined or a costly one. They want grace but
they want it cheaply as Dietrich Bonhoeffer once said. I'm sure they
mean well, but the fact is that they are sanitizing Christology and
stage-managing Christ in a manner that is unacceptable to the integrity
of the Gospel and to the Lord's own self-understanding.

Then there are others, in our time as in Paul's time, who pro-
fess to be Christian but whose de facto lives make them "enemies
of the cross of Christ." Paul describes such Christians as the ones who
"will end in disaster! Their god is their belly and their glory is in their
shame. I am talking about those who are set upon the things of this
world" (Philemon 3:18–19). Perhaps we know some of them. Perhaps
we ourselves are tempted at times to become some of them.

Jesus says, "Whoever wishes to come after me must deny
himself; take up his cross, and follow me." William Barclay, in his commentary, places these words "near the heart and center of the Christian
faith." And he says that we will understand their demands only if we
take the words "very simply and literally." There is no authentic Christ
without a suffering messiah and there is no glory without the cross.
Barclay continues: "If [one] will follow Jesus Christ he must ever say
no to himself and yes to Christ. He must say no to his own natural
love of ease and comfort. He must say no to every course of action
based on self-seeking and self-will.

He must say no to the instincts and the desires which prompt
him to touch and taste and handle forbidden things. He must unhesi-
tatingly say yes to the voice and the command of Jesus Christ. He
must be able to say with Paul that it is no longer he who lives but Christ
who lives in him. He lives no longer to follow his own will, but to
follow the will of Christ, and in that service he finds perfect freedom"
(*The Gospel of Mark: The New Daily Study Bible,* Nashville, TN:
Westminster John Knox Press, 2001).

# 134B Twenty-fifth Sunday in Ordinary Time

## MARK 9:30–37

### Defined by Service

In his inaugural address on January 20, 1961, President John F. Kennedy said, "And so, my fellow Americans: ask not what your country can do for you—ask what you can do for your country. My fellow citizens of the world: ask not what America will do for you, but what together we can do for the freedom of man." On the death of the British prime minister Lord Curzon (1925), his political opponent Stanley Baldwin said, "He pursued no other course than that of doing his duty where it was decided he could best render service."

In everybody's estimate, Jesus himself must be reckoned among history's greatest servants. For us Christians, of course, there was no greater servant of God or greater servant of others than Jesus. It is in the context of service that we consider today's Gospel message.

Our Lord is slowly making his way to Jerusalem. There he will surrender his life for us in a final act of service. It is, therefore, critical that his chosen apostles have a clear understanding of the message of salvation that he has been teaching them through word and example for nearly three years. For these apostles are the ones he must rely upon to continue his mission and ministry when he returns to the Father in glory. The apostles are, instead, caught up in their own self-interest and self-promotion. Our Lord senses this and he asks, "What were you arguing about on the way?" Like a gang of thieves caught red-handed, they fall silent. I'd like to think that they were speechless with embarrassment. I'd like to think that all of a sudden they realized how small they were and how unworthy their ambitions were.

Here is their Lord on his way to endure the humility of public execution, and here are his chosen apostles arguing over which of them is the greatest in God's kingdom, a kingdom which for them is still a misunderstood one of power and grandeur.

Bible scholar Wilfrid Harrington, in his commentary on Mark (*Mark: New Testament Message—A Biblical-Theological Commentary*, Collegeville, MN: Michael Glazier, 1979), notes that the Aramaic word used by Jesus for a child is *talya*. In Aramaic, it is also the word for "servant." Our Lord links the two meanings of the same word. The child thus represents the least and most vulnerable in the community. A true disciple of Jesus "receives" the child; i.e., accepts the responsibility of service to the least and the most vulnerable. For it is in serving the least that one is the greatest in the kingdom of God.

For all the economic prosperity that has marked, as a whole, the years since the Second World War, the gap continues to widen between the rich and the poor all over the world. For multitudes, justice still seems to depend on who has the best connections and who can afford the most expensive lawyers. Perhaps it was always this way. Even those of us not classed in the ranks of the officially poor experience hardship at times as we try to match our small pension or our social security check with the fairly high cost of living of a rather simple lifestyle. These forms of poverty, and other forms of vulnerability in society, stand in need of service; and, not least in need of service, is the spiritual poverty of the fallen-away and the unchurched in our land.

The Christian is defined by service. In the face of the pastoral challenges before us today, there must be no room for talk of precedence among Christians, nor must there be any shuffling for position and prominence in the contemporary Church. Our Lord does not allow it, and the urgency of the Gospel message has no time for it.

There is an immense apostolate of service all around us and, in the abandonment of the faith in our time, the apostolate is growing by the day. What we need is the grace that takes hold of us at our core and shakes us into action. What we need to pray for is the seal of Jesus on our hearts. It is the seal that reads, "If anyone wishes to be first, he shall be the last of all and the servant of all."

# 137B Twenty-sixth Sunday in Ordinary Time

## MARK 9:38–43, 45, 47–48

### At What Price?

In the time of the Cold War (1961), President Kennedy said that our country would "pay any price" to preserve its liberty and its democratic ideals, and "shoulder any burden" in order to expand freedom and human rights in the world. These words were directed at the Soviet Union.

All of us have ideals. It's hard to live a meaningful life without them. And all the ideals have their price tags. Jesus, too, had his ideals. And they had their price tags. The price tags were these: our Lord's ideals reduced his time on earth to little more than three decades and they cost him the loss of many disciples (cf. John 6:66) and, eventually, his own life on the cross.

In today's Gospel, our Lord mentions two great ideals, and he wants us to share them with him. They are that we live his life of grace now in the kingdom of God, and that we enjoy the state of glory with him in heaven later.

What does living in the kingdom of God mean? It means living out God's will in our lives as taught to us by Jesus. It's the only way to live. Jesus calls it "life"—real life.

Saint Paul says that "to live is Christ" (Philemon 1:21). The saints call it living virtuously, or living in the state of grace, or living at peace with God and others. Living in the kingdom in this manner progresses into living with God in glory in the hereafter. What price does this living in Christ demand of us?

The first thing we should say is that any talk of price or price tags or cost is only used to emphasize the worth and the beauty and the inner joy of living life with Christ. Second, our Lord's words about cutting off our hand or our leg or plucking out our eye, if they lead us to sin, is only meant to stress the priority of living life according to

God's will and not our own. For our will is sin-prone. Left to itself it always gets us into trouble. But following God's will always keeps us out of trouble, and away from the heartbreak that following our sin-prone will causes us and causes others who are impacted by our selfish behavior.

The vivid imagery that Jesus uses in relation to the hand and the leg and the eye is taken from the teaching language of the rabbis of his time. Sin is not an act of the hand or the leg or the eye as such, but of the will. The will uses the body as its agent in order to externalize its sin. Hence, according to scripture scholar William Barclay, the rabbis had sayings that named the various body parts which the will uses to materialize its sins. They said such things as, "The eye and the heart are the brokers of sin" and "The eye and the heart are the handmaids of sin" (*The Gospel of Mark: The New Daily Study Bible*, Nashville, TN: Westminster John Knox Press, 2001).

The Gospel message today is an exhortation. And it is a straightforward one. Living our lives in Christ, and in the sure hope of glory, is worth its price tag; worth the cost of any sacrifice such living may require of us.

# 140B Twenty-seventh Sunday in Ordinary Time

## MARK 10:2−16 (LONGER) OR MARK 10:2−12 (SHORTER)

### Like a Child

There are two separate but related lessons for us in today's Gospel. One has to do with our attitude toward children and women; the other has to do with the quality of our personal faith.

Scripture scholars Wilfrid Harrington and William Barclay, in their respective Marcan commentaries, tell us that it was customary for Jewish mothers to bring their children to a great rabbi or a prophet for a blessing. Usually, this happened on the occasion of the child's birthday. It is for doing this that the disciples "rebuked" the mothers in today's Gospel incident. Our Lord is "indignant" at the disciples' behavior even if, as we may suppose, they were only trying to protect him from the bother and noise of these children and their mothers. "Let the children come to me; do not prevent them," Jesus says, "for the kingdom of God belongs to such as these."

What does Jesus mean by saying that the kingdom of God belongs to such as children? Wilfrid Harrington answers, "The kingdom is a gift which must be received with simplicity" (*Mark: New Testament Message—A Biblical-Theological Commentary*, Collegeville, MN: Michael Glazier, 1979). We adults, on the other hand, tend to bring a lot of baggage and conditions with us when we accept the kingdom. According to Tertullian (an early Christian writer of the late-second and early-third centuries), the early Christians used this incident as a justification of infant Baptism and, I suppose, it helped lay the foundation for the rather central position that children have occupied in the Church's liturgy, sacraments, and catechesis down through the generations. Harrington says that when Jesus blessed the children he did so "fervently" (as indicated by Mark's use of a strengthened form of the verb, to bless). In this way, he says, "the Church is shown how it is to treat children."

The Jewish writer Isaac Bashevis Singer has spent his life exploring our relationship with God in his novels and stories. Our relationship suffers precisely because it is adult and complicated, unlike that of the child. In his Nobel Prize acceptance speech in 1978 he observed: "Children [unlike we adults] don't read to find their identity, to free themselves from guilt, to quench the thirst for rebellion, or to get rid of alienation. They have no use for psychology. They detest sociology. They still believe in God, the family, angels, devils, logic, clarity . . . and other such obsolete stuff." It is only when we leave childhood and enter adulthood that we become sophisticated and ambitious and cunning and, as William Wordsworth noted in his poem, "Ode to the Intimations of Immortality," the "shades of the prison-house begin to close" upon us. Jesus, obviously, was well aware of this difference between the simplicity of the innocent child and the complexity of the sinful adult.

So, Jesus uses the child to teach us a lesson about membership in the kingdom of God, and about the qualities of simplicity and childlike trust in God that our faith must possess. God is our Father and we are his children. Our approach to God, then, must have the qualities of the little child at home—humility, obedience, dependence, pliability, and, above all else, simplicity and loving trust. For the child is one who "still believes the best of others and has not yet learned to suspect the world" (Barclay).

We who are adults do not and cannot live in the world as children. For we have learned adult cunning through life's harsh realities. But we can and must live as children in our Father's house. We can and must live the relationship with God as utterly trusting children in the presence of their utterly loving Father. And if you trawl through your own life's experience, you will admit that God, your most trustworthy Father, is nowhere to be found among those who have hurt you or harmed your life's passage.

# 143B Twenty-eighth Sunday in Ordinary Time

## MARK 10:17–30; (LONGER) OR MARK 10:17–27 (SHORTER)

### Prioritize the Kingdom!

Riches do not of themselves exclude anyone from the kingdom of God. For example, Joseph of Arimathea was a wealthy man and a friend of Jesus, and Jesus was buried in his tomb. Nevertheless, according to Jesus it is hard for people of wealth to enter the kingdom of God. Why? Perhaps because it is hard for them to accept the conditions of Christian living. These conditions include total trust in God, not in wealth, and a giving rather than a hoarding heart.

In addition, wealth carries with it the responsibility of investing it well. This can be a great source of spiritual distraction and of worry. Maybe this is why the economist John Kenneth Galbraith observes in his *Age of Uncertainty* (Boston: Houghton-Mifflin, 1978), that money "ranks with love as man's greatest source of joy, and with death as his greatest source of anxiety."

We know from social history that many people make a moral mess of their lives because of wealth and the pursuit of wealth. They grow old stripped of their good name and of what should be the tranquil evening years of their lives because of imprisonment, penalties, or adverse publicity. To quote Ovid in their regard, "plenty has made me poor" (*Metamorphoses,* III).

Jewish religion blessed wealth. It was a sign of God's favor, but in today's Gospel, our Lord warns against it. Scripture scholar William Barclay tells us that the amazement of the disciples at Jesus' words stems from this seeming contradiction between Jewish teaching and Christ's teaching. "They would have argued," says Barclay, "that the more prosperous the man was, the more certain he was of entry into the Kingdom" (*The Gospel of Mark: The New Daily Study Bible,* Nashville, TN: Westminster John Knox Press, 2001).

Today, the pursuit of wealth is as committed an enterprise among the general population as it used to be mostly among the so-called upper crust. We feel as blessed in our wealth today as did the religious Jews of old or the church-going master from the big plantation. We are heavy into consumerism, into goods and appliances and acquisitions of all sorts. We really don't know what to do with half of the stuff we accumulate. We would be easy targets for a prophet's condemnation.

But such condemnation would miss the point of today's Gospel. Our Lord does not condemn wealth. Nor does he measure the materialist's psyche. Nor does he quantify the amount of goods and property that a follower of his may possess. Nor does he say that the rich cannot possibly enter the kingdom of God, and that they are incapable of living the Christian life. He points out, instead, the additional difficulties that wealth brings to the already demanding Christian enterprise: the distraction, the worry and, above all else, the risk of a divided heart.

Let us, then, not waste our time in useless condemnation of wealth but commit ourselves to the wise guideline, and to the priority of interest, that our Lord gives us in Matthew's Gospel when he says, "Seek first the kingdom of God and his righteousness [his reign over your heart], and all these things will be given you besides" (Matthew 6:33).

# 146B Twenty-ninth Sunday in Ordinary Time

## Mark 10:35–45 (longer) or Mark 10:42–45 (shorter)

### A Different Standard

In their request to Jesus, James and John are trying to get a step ahead of the other apostles. They are very ambitious in their request. They want the top places in Christ's kingdom. They want the most senior positions in his cabinet. "One at your right and the other at your left" were the same words used by their mother when she made the same request of Jesus for her two boys (Matthew 20:21). Our Lord turns them down. Is Christ condemning ambition? Not really. The dictionary tells me that ambition is a strong desire to achieve something that is great or good. Now the coming of the kingdom of God is a great and a good thing, and Jesus himself desired it with all his heart. In the Church, in later years, Paul will tell Timothy that whoever ambitions the office of Bishop—whoever aspires to a position of high authority in the Church—"desires a noble task" (1 Timothy 3:1). The Lord, then, is not condemning ambition in its good sense.

There is, however, another kind of desire for power or distinction. This is selfish ambition. Such ambition seems to have been the ambition of James and John. Humans handle inordinate ambition poorly.

So, Jesus "summoned" the apostles to him. There is a certain urgency in the tone of that verb. And the scholars know why. It is only a short time since Jesus last spoke to the apostles about receiving the kingdom with the simplicity of a child. It is only a short time since he last spoke to them about being the servants of the kingdom. It is only a short time since he last spoke to them about not making the work of the kingdom their vocation to the exclusion of everybody else (see Mark 9:38–41). All of these things that he has so recently said to them seem to have merely passed in through one ear and straight out the other. The disciples have not listened to him at all! So, he "summons" them and starts, as it were, all over again on the issue of simplicity and service in the kingdom of God.

He tells them that the question of "who sits where" in glory is for the Father to decide. It is not for Jesus to decide, and it is not for the disciples to ambition or to argue over. The Father's arrangement of places in the kingdom, we may assume, is based on our love of Jesus, our service to others, and our commitment to the spread of the kingdom on earth.

Our Lord goes further. The kingdom of God, he says, follows a very different standard from that which obtains in the kingdoms of the earth, and in their structures of authority. Among the non-believers, he says, authority means power. And power is used to lord it over people. "It shall not be so among you," Jesus says. It shall not be that way in the Church! Or in the community of our parish! Nor shall it be that way for Christians who serve in political life, in the social services, in health care. Nor shall it be that way for Christians in the privacy of their homes, or where they work, or where they teach, or in their dealings with the poor and the homeless and the migrant workers.

For, in following Christ, we Christians follow a different standard from that which obtains in the world. It is the standard of humility, simplicity, and of selfless service. And it applies everywhere we are, and everywhere we take ourselves.

Scripture scholar William Barclay observes that in Christ's theology greatness consists "not in reducing others to one's service but in reducing oneself to their service" (*The Gospel of Mark: The New Daily Study Bible,* Nashville, TN: Westminster John Knox Press, 2001). The test is not, he says, "What service can I extract?" but "What service can I give?"

# 149B Thirtieth Sunday in Ordinary Time

## MARK 10:46–52

### A Grammar of Discipleship

Jesus is on his way to celebrate the Passover in Jerusalem. It is destined to be his last Passover. The road to Jerusalem passes through the town of Jericho. Passover is a major Jewish feast, so the road is jammed with pilgrims on their way to Jerusalem for the feast.

At this late stage in his life, Jesus is a well-known personality. The Gospel says that he and his disciples are joined on the way by a sizable crowd of pilgrims. No doubt many pilgrims are eager to catch every word of his teaching. No doubt, on the other hand, there are many in Jericho—a dormitory town for many of the temple's priests—who have long since made up their minds about this upstart rabbi who would destroy their temple and their traditions. They have stopped their ears and shut their eyes to this young rabbi and to his new teaching.

As Jesus and the disciples and the multitude of pilgrims continue on their pilgrimage, they pass a blind man begging by the roadside. Suddenly, he interrupts the Lord's teaching with cries for pity. Everyone rebukes him. But that only makes him cry out all the more. Jesus eventually says, "Call him." As soon as he is called he fires off his cloak and springs up. He speaks with a minimum of words: "Master, I want to see."

Mark constructs the scene so that we may see the contrast between the temple priests' lack of faith in Jesus and the ardent faith of this beggar by the roadside. Our Lord answers the blind man's request precisely because of his blinding faith. In this, Mark wishes us to see the contrast between the blindness of the temple priests with regard to Jesus and the humble insight of poor Bartimaeus. Then Jesus tells Bartimaeus that he may now go on his way. But the way that Bartimaeus chooses to go is not his own way; he chooses to follow

Jesus' way. Jesus' way is not only the physical way to Jerusalem but, more so, the way of Christ's teaching and of Christian fellowship.

We are aware of the fact that "the way" is early Christian code for the way of the Lord, or Christian discipleship. Scripture scholar William Barclay suggests that the conditions of discipleship are illustrated in this scene involving Bartimaeus. First, there is the man's desire to meet Jesus. Then there is his persistence. And when Jesus calls him his response is immediate. He knows exactly what he wants of the Lord. He may not be all that sure how to address Jesus properly, but there is nothing unsure about his faith in the Lord and in what Jesus can do. Then in response to the Lord's goodness, he is full of gratitude. And he does not hesitate to follow the Lord and his way. All of these conditions, or strands, make up the steps of conversion and are a grammar of discipleship.

Bartimaeus does not elect to walk his own selfish way. He does not elect to languish by the roadside of life as it passes by. As soon as he gets the opportunity he makes the way of the Lord the way of life for him. May it continue to be our way through life as well.

# 152B Thirty-first Sunday in Ordinary Time

## MARK 12:28B–34

### Effective Love

Life is lived under law; otherwise we live in chaos. The trouble is that when there are too many laws there is another kind of chaos. One cannot function in this chaos without the aid of an army of legal experts, interpreters, consultants, and lawyers.

The scribes and the Sadducees were among this army of lawyers and experts in our Lord's time. Their business was to interpret the Law of God for the people. Some of them expanded the Law to cover every possible human situation, even to the point of making the Law

scarcely tolerable for ordinary folk. Others tried to reduce the Law
to its basics, or to its fundamental principles. There was, therefore, in
Judaism what Bible scholar William Barclay calls "a double tendency."

Many laws, which some might consider minor, had the
stature of commandments for others. We should not be surprised
then when, in today's Gospel, a scribe comes up to Jesus looking for
clarification—looking for the fundamentals of his faith. He asks Jesus,
"Which is the first of all the commandments?" He is asking, in effect,
"What is the essence of the Law? What is the heart of our religion?"
Jesus answers, "Love God with your whole being, and love your
neighbor as yourself." Our Lord puts God first, but ties our neighbor
to him. Many years later John, the beloved disciple, will write, "If
anyone says, 'I love God,' but hates his brother, he is a liar; for whoever
does not love a brother whom he has seen cannot love God he has
not seen. This is the commandment we have from him: whoever loves
God must also love his brother" (1 John 4:20–21).

Saint Vincent de Paul is one of our best models of loving
God and our neighbor and, specifically, of loving God through our
neighbor. While the one is not the other with Vincent, he makes
it quite clear that the one cannot be divorced from the other. Vincent
battled against the image of a harsh God. The Jansenists of his time
were presenting such a God to the people of France, and especially to
the illiterate poor. In its place, Vincent promoted the God of love. We
see this illustrated in the incident in which he counseled one poor
soul who had lost both parents that "God will take the place of a
father and a mother for you." And to his friend and co-worker Saint
Louise de Marillac, he wrote, "God is love and he wishes us to go to
him by love."

How did Vincent himself go to God by love? He personally
chose to love the least loved and the most unlovable of his time.
Among the former were the illiterate rural poor, and among the latter
were the galley slaves whose cause he took up and to whom he minis-
tered personally. He became their chaplain, as he had once been
chaplain at the royal court.

You and I live in comparative affluence. The economy is still
sound despite the tragedy of September 11, 2001, and its economic
fallout. Some people describe our society as a very affluent one.
And that is fine. But you and I are aware of the fact that there are gaps

in our economic blessedness. Many of our people live below the poverty line. There is also considerable psychological poverty. And there is spiritual poverty too.

We see, perhaps even among family members and friends, the increasing numbers of people who are spiritually impoverished and who live without God's "connections of love"; namely, his word and his sacraments. We should pray over these various forms of impoverishment among our neighbors. We should pray over what we might be able to do to alleviate them.

The scholars tell us that no one in Jewish theology thought of joining together, in a radical or root sense, the commandments of loving God and loving our neighbor until Jesus arrived and made a firm connection. We are the heirs to this connection that Jesus made. We should ask God, then, for the grace to address our neighbor's needs with a loving heart wherever and whenever we possibly can.

# 155B Thirty-second Sunday in Ordinary Time

## MARK 12:38–44 (LONGER) OR MARK 12:41–44 (SHORTER)

### Out on a Limb

Poverty is a terrible state to be in. The character Undershaft, in George Bernard Shaw's play *Major Barbara*, says, "Poverty is the worst of all crimes. All the other crimes are virtues beside it." In a personal memoir, the Academy Award winning actor Spencer Tracy said of his early, poverty-driven days, "There were times my pants were so thin I could sit on a dime and tell if it was heads or tails." The dime is, of course, the thinnest of our coins, even thinner than the cent. The widow's small copper coins in today's Gospel are called in Greek the *lepta*, meaning the thin ones. The lepton was the thinnest of the Roman coins.

One aspect of poverty is the insecurity that comes with it. Becoming a widow in ancient times normally meant entering a state of social and financial insecurity—and, perhaps worst of all, a state of psychological insecurity. (Is this why the apostle James says in his letter, "Religion that is pure and undefiled before God is this: to care for orphans and widows in their affliction and to keep one's self unstained by the world" [1:27]?)

The woman that our Lord observes putting money into the temple treasury is a widow. Some wealthy people are putting in money too. They put in big amounts. The widow puts in only two small coins. They are worth a few cents. It is all that she has. Our Lord calls the disciples to himself and tells them that this poor widow has actually given more than the others. For they gave out of their surplus: she gave out of her poverty. In fact, she has given all she had—her last bit of security.

Bible scholar Wilfrid Harrington says that this widow "had let go of every shred of security and had committed herself wholly to God." And Harrington notes that what the Lord says to his apostles through this episode is "his final word on discipleship" (*Mark: New Testament Message—A Biblical-Theological Commentary*, Collegeville, MN: Michael Glazier, 1979).

Maybe the widow's action, and our Lord's approval of it, puts two challenges before us. The first is this. Are we, the Lord's modern-day disciples, being told that our giving should be not only generous but even sacrificial? The amount we actually give doesn't matter; but what it costs us personally or sacrificially does. Perhaps we give only because we have a lot, or because someone is pestering us, or because it is expected of us. Such giving has never made us penniless, or threatened our psychology with insecurity.

Second, we are challenged to be more conscious of the fact that our giving, whether of time, of talent, or of treasure, is an instrument of identification with the Lord who gave his all for us. He left us an example through this poor widow and through his own life. He is the One who came to serve rather than to be served. He is the One who had nowhere to lay his head. He is the One who lived in earthly insecurity as proof of his commitment to us and reliance on the Father. And he is the One who ends his disciples' seminary formation program with this touching episode of the widow who, in giving almost nothing, gave everything to her God.

# 158B Thirty-third Sunday in Ordinary Time

## MARK 13:24–32

### Living in Hope

The thirteenth chapter of Mark's Gospel, from which our Gospel reading today is taken, begins with Jesus saying to the apostles, "See that no one deceives you" (v. 5) and ends with him saying, "What I say to you, I say to all: "Watch!" (v. 37). Our Lord's words are intended for us, too, as the latest generation of his followers. What does he want us not to be deceived by, and what are we to watch for? We are in the "end times"—as this present period of history is popularly called by some.

Jesus is coming back soon. We do not know the day or the hour of his coming. Neither did Jesus, according to his own words. But some people think they know the precise day and hour. Some people even think that they themselves are the prophets appointed to herald his immanent return. It is of these that Jesus says, "See that no one deceives you" (v. 5), and he continues: "False messiahs and false prophets will arise and will perform signs and wonders in order to mislead, if that were possible, the elect. Be watchful! I have told it all to you beforehand" (vv. 22–23).

Jesus also asks us to take heed of a series of images which mark the stages of the "end times," and which will precede his coming. There is some confusion over these images. It will help us if we realize that the "end times"—as Mark aligns them—come as a series of phases, set in sequence. For our purposes here, let us collapse the phases into three.

First comes the destruction of the temple and of Jerusalem. This event subsequently occurred in 70 AD. Next follows a set of signs by which we may know that Christ's return is a) close and b) at hand. Finally, as the signs progress and are fulfilled, our watchfulness for the coming of the Lord must increase for he is at the point of arrival or may even be "knocking at the door" (Revelation 3:20).

We poor humans love the sensational. We find it hard to confine ourselves to the slow pace of normal life and of faithful Christian living. We long for the unusual and the extraordinary. We are always looking for signs and miracles, as Jesus said of the people of his own generation (cf. John 4:48). This is the reason why, I suppose, more people read the tabloids than the daily local newspapers. We gather around our coffee tables for a "buzz session" where the best news is the most sensational news, and we glory in our gossip as if we were sharing gospel truth. In line with this yen for the sensational, every generation produces preachers and people who latch onto the destructive imagery of the "end times" and make predictions about the exact day and hour of the end. In recent years it has become a huge religious industry.

Jesus says in the last line of today's Gospel, "But of that day or hour, no one knows, neither the angels in heaven, nor the Son, but only the Father." It was not permitted to Jesus to know the exact day or hour of his return to us. So why do Christians waste their time trying to predict it?

Our Lord's words infer that the exact timing of his return is of no consequence to our present spiritual journey or to our future destiny. What is of consequence is our watchfulness and our preparedness for the joy of his return. What is of consequence is our good use of the remaining time and of its opportunities for grace and goodness.

# Solemnities and Feasts of the Lord and Saints

# 161B Last Sunday in Ordinary Time

Our Lord Jesus Christ the King
Thirty-fourth Sunday in Ordinary Time

## JOHN 18:33B–37

### Summoned by Love

I suppose each generation searches for love more than it searches for anything else. It seems to me that it doesn't matter what century or which culture one looks at; the poetry and the songs of all the generations are the same. They are the poetry and the songs of love.

"Love makes the world go 'round," says a popular song. We know this to be a fact. We know it in our bones. Our need for love is at the core of us, and love is the core of God. Love is where we unite with God. The French playwright Jean Anouilh observes: "Love is, above all, the gift of oneself" (*Ardele Ou La Marguerite Suivi De La*, Paris: Gallimard). And who better than God in Jesus to prove it.

Today's Gospel passage is taken from John's Gospel. Saint John, as you know, is called the beloved disciple, or the disciple of love. Of the Gospel writers, John has the fullest (and by far the longest) description of what transpired at the Last Supper and what Jesus said in the course of it. What went on there and what was said there centers on love. "I give you a new commandment: love one another. As I have loved you, so you also should love one another. This is how all will know that you are my disciples, if you have love for one another" (John 13:34–35). The badge of the Christian is love. "I give you a new commandment: love one another" (v. 34).

In today's Gospel Jesus tells Pilate that he came into the world to witness to the truth. The truth of which he speaks includes—massively—the truth of God's enduring love for us. It is the truth of God's saving love for us. For "God so loved the world that he gave his only Son, so that everyone who believes in him might not perish but might have eternal life" (John 3:16). The biblical scholar Michael Mullins includes, in the truth about which Jesus speaks to Pilate, his "revelation" of the Father's "faithful loving kindness" (*The Gospel of John: A Commentary,* Blackrock, Co. Dublin: Columba Press, 2004).

The kingship that Jesus attributes to himself is, then, a kingship of love. And the kingdom of which he is king is the kingdom of love. It is presently inhabited by those who have been saved through his Father's loving design and his own sacrificial love. And the kingdom is the Church, the gathering of those who try to love one another as selflessly as Jesus loved them. Jesus is the king of love. He is the king of hearts.

Carlo Carretto writes: "All the loves that we discover and experience one by one in the course of existence . . . are only partial stages preparing . . . that total, holy love which is the fulfillment of all loves: love of God, which will be our heritage forever, the devouring fire of our paradise. Then we shall understand why we were born, why God has summoned us into existence" (*Summoned by Love,* Maryknoll, NY: Orbis Books, 1978). In other words, we have been summoned into existence by the God of Love in order to love and, in our loving, to prepare ourselves for the everlasting love of heaven.

# 165B The Most Holy Trinity

## Sunday After Pentecost

## MATTHEW 28:16–20

## Companions on the Road

This is Trinity Sunday. Some years ago, a celebrity athlete left the Church amid the usual media hullabaloo. When asked why he was taking this step he said that he could no longer believe in a "three-headed God." He was referring to the Blessed Trinity, our belief that God is a God of three divine Persons.

Now the Church doesn't believe in a three-headed God either, so there is no reason to leave the Church over the Blessed Trinity. But I suppose that the celebrity athlete was revealing the picture of God that he had held in his head since childhood. It is a picture that some of us, perhaps, still hold.

The God that Christ revealed to us is not a three-headed God, nor is God three Gods running around each doing his own thing. There is only one God. That one God is God as our Father, God as our Savior, and God as our Sanctifier. God as Father created us as his children. God as Savior redeemed us when we fell from grace through Adam's original sin and our own personal sins. God as Spirit energizes us in the passages of life through his inspiration and his grace. God does all of this, according to Saint Paul, so that we may grow into the likeness of God's beloved Son and "be filled with all the fullness of God" (Ephesians 3:19).

Some of us may experience difficulty in praying to God. We wonder who we should address our prayers to. Should we address them to the Father, or to the Son, or to the Holy Spirit? Jesus addressed his prayers to God the Father. The official and liturgical prayers of the Church are also addressed to the Father, through the Son, and in the power of the Spirit.

Our private prayers will normally address the divine Person whom we feel is most appropriate to the need or the intention at hand. If, for example, we find our hearts full of gratitude for the wonders of creation, or for a great harvest, or for a glorious day at the beach, we may find ourselves thanking God the Creator and Father of these gifts.

If we find ourselves struggling with personal suffering or sin or loneliness in our lives, we may find ourselves leaning on Jesus, the Suffering Servant and Savior. If we need encouragement and inspiration for our teaching, our office work, our housework, our homework, or for our computing and creative enterprises, we may turn to God the Spirit and Energizer. There is no hard and fast rule in this matter of addressing our prayers to God. It is mainly a question of which divine Person suits us best as we try to focus our hearts and center our needs on God. And so it is with the Trinity. Each divine Person is fully God and each is "the supreme reality of God," as the Fourth Lateran Council (1215 AD) puts it.

And when we try to focus our hearts and center our prayers, we do well to remember that the three divine Persons are not "up there" in the heavens but down here in our hearts. For the Trinity "indwells" in us through grace, and "we are the temple of the living God" (2 Corinthians 6:16).

There is a certain harmony (the old writers called it congruence) in the fact that God is three divine Persons and that they correspond to the three levels of salvation. God as Creator and Father put us on the road of life. God as Savior puts us back on the road when we go off it through sin. God as Spirit directs the journey that is not yet finished but that will end, God willing, where it all began— in the Godhead. Let us walk our road today and tomorrow and every day confidently, in the name of the Father, and of the Son, and of the Holy Spirit. Amen.

# 168B The Most Holy Body and Blood of Christ

### Sunday after Trinity Sunday

## MARK 14:12–16, 22–26

### Source and Summit

"The Eucharist is the source and summit of the Christian life," says the *Catechism of the Catholic Church* (CCC, 1324) quoting the Second Vatican Council (*Lumen gentium*, 11). "The Eucharist is the heart and summit of the Church's life" (#1407).

In my experience of the catechumenate (or "convert work" as we once called it), the Catholic understanding of the Eucharist is one of the most attractive aspects of our faith to many people coming to Catholicism from a Christian background. In my experience of parish ministry, trying to live one's life without being able to receive the Eucharist is the stimulus for many Catholics to rectify an invalid marriage. I was still wet behind the ears when a parishioner came to me in tears with her invalid marriage and said, "I just have to have my marriage blessed. I can't go on living without Holy Communion."

Our Church's restriction on non-Catholic Christians receiving communion at the Eucharistic Liturgy is more than posturing by intransigent Church leaders: it signals the central importance of the Eucharist to every thinking Christian and our mutual desire to understand it and to celebrate it as Christ intended.

But of at least equal pastoral concern to our Bishops ought to be the fact that many Catholics seem to know less than they realize about their Church's teaching on the Eucharist. In fact, many Catholics these days understand the Eucharist more or less as many non-Catholic Christians do. Neither group seems to understand the Eucharist as our expression of that sacred action whereby Jesus established the new covenant in his blood. And neither group has much sense of the Eucharist as the reenactment of the Last Supper, and of how that can be so. At any rate, that's my experience from my teaching and from discussion groups. This short homily is not the place to address all of these critical matters.

Let us take a look instead at our understanding of another aspect of the Eucharist—the real presence of the Lord therein. Many young Catholics these days understand the real presence as—no more than—"receiving Jesus in a special way." Whatever the good intention behind this phrase, identifying the eucharistic presence of Jesus as his presence "in a special way" is hardly an advance on the old symbolic, spiritual, and hidden presence phraseologies of the Reformation debates.

Pope Paul VI pointed out (in *Mysterium Fidei*) that even the term *real presence* is not a sufficient description of Christ's presence in the Eucharist, and that reserving the term to describe Christ's presence in the Eucharist tends to minimize the reality of his presence with us in many other ways. For Christ is really present in other ways besides the Eucharist. He is really present in his indwelling in us. He is really present where two or three Christians, of any denomination, gather in his name. He is really present in his word in scripture. He is really present in the action of each sacrament. He is really present in the poor. His real presence in the Eucharist is to be understood, writes the Pope, as the "whole and entire" presence of Christ.

Such a presence of Christ in the Eucharist is not adequately expressed by the phrase "real presence," and far less by "symbolic presence" and "spiritual presence" and "hidden presence" and—now—"present in a special way."

The *Catechism of the Catholic Church* quotes the Council of Trent in its own comprehensive description of Christ's presence in the Eucharist: "Christ himself is present, living and glorious, in a true, real and substantial manner, his body and his blood, with his soul and divinity" (CCC, 1413). Perhaps both council and catechism are trying to tell us that, whereas all presences of Christ are real, absolutely nothing of the fullness of Christ is absent from his eucharistic presence.

You and I encounter the Lord in the Eucharist with a fullness of presence that is unique and that lacks nothing, on his part, of reality, intensity, and intimacy. The only encounter with the Lord that outdoes the eucharistic encounter will be our meeting together in heaven in the state of mutual glory. In our present pilgrim condition, the Eucharist is, quite simply, our summit meeting and his summit presence.

# 621 The Assumption of the Blessed Virgin Mary

**August 14 / At the Vigil Mass**

## LUKE 11:27–28

### First Things First

The spiritual writer Carlo Carretto describes the time before the Second Vatican Council as a time when important spiritual realities sometimes played second string to less important ones. It was a time, he writes, when people's faith was nourished "with the pap of devotions rather than with the mighty strength of the word of God"

(*Summoned by Love,* Maryknoll, NY: Orbis Books, 1979). Perhaps his observation is a little too one-sided. There is a place for devotional practices. Devotional practices should flow from the liturgy and the word of God. If the devotional practices cease to lead us to the word of God and the liturgy of the Eucharist, then they have lost their charism. At any rate, he is making the point that the People of God are primarily and authentically fashioned in the faith by attention to the word of God rather than through devotional practices. Carretto stresses the preeminence of the word of God in Christian formation.

Jesus, in the Gospel of this evening's liturgy, also stresses the preeminence of the word of God. To the woman in the crowd who blesses his mother, Jesus replies, "Rather, blessed are those who hear the word of God and observe it." He is telling the woman, and you and me, that "attentiveness to God's word is more important than bio-logical relationship to [him]" (from, footnote 8, Luke 11:27–28, *New American Bible*).

There is a parallel scene in Mark's Gospel where Jesus is told that his mother and brothers and sisters are outside the house looking for him. He looks around at the people who are gathered in his presence, and who are listening carefully to his words, and says, "Here are my mother and my brothers. For whoever does the will of God is my brother and sister and mother" (Mark 3:34–35).

Bible scholar Wilfrid Harrington sees in these words of Jesus the distinction between "those who stand outside the sphere of sal-vation and those who are within it. Those outside, though they be the Lord's own people, his own kin, are those who do not recognize that his ministry is the work of God. Those within are they who do the will of God, who recognize and accept the ministry of Jesus and gather about him in faith and discipleship" (*Mark: New Testament Message / A Biblical-Theological Commentary,* Collegeville, MN: Michael Glazier, 1979).

New Testament scholar Philip Van Linden notes the likely cost of doing God's will and living by the word of God: "Jesus expects his followers to have the same single-minded dedication to God's will as he does. Such dedication may lead to conflicts . . ." (*The Gospel According to Mark: The Collegeville Bible Commentary,* Collegeville, MN: Liturgical Press, 1984). "Blood ties," writes theologian Elizabeth A. Johnson, "do not guarantee a place in [Jesus'] community of disciples, but loving and acting on behalf of the reign of God do. (*Truly Our Sister: A Theology of Mary in the Communion of Saints*, New York: Continuum, 2003).

In Mary, the mother of Jesus, we have the example of one who was eminently attentive to the word of God. She always acted upon that word and was wholly fashioned by it. With Mary, it was always a matter of hearing God's pleasure and of "Thy will be done."

You and I wish to follow Mary's example. She is the pattern for our pilgrim lives. We wish to discern God's will in our lives, and for all our choices and decisions. We wish to grow in grace by growing in the knowledge of the Lord. How shall we grow surely and authentically in that knowledge? Here, at the Liturgy of the Word, is a good place to learn and a good place to grow.

May we, then, always listen attentively to "the word of the Lord" and "the gospel of the Lord" and find our discernment and our direction in them. Let Mary's attitude be our attitude toward God's holy, directing, and transforming word. Her transformation ended in her glorious assumption into heaven. Ours will too, even though our body, unlike hers, must first return to the dust out of which it was formed.

# 622 The Assumption of the Blessed Virgin Mary

**August 15 / Mass during the Day**

## LUKE 1:39–56

### Our Pattern

The thanksgiving hymn of Mary in today's Gospel is well-known to us as the Magnificat, or Mary's Song. It is modeled on Hannah's Song in 1 Samuel: 2:1–10, and some of its lines are direct quotations. Mary speaks her song of thanksgiving when her cousin Elizabeth calls her blessed for her trust in God that his word to her would be fulfilled.

Scripture scholar William Barclay calls the Magnificat not only a thanksgiving song but a revolutionary song. Jesus' Beatitudes later on will be classed revolutionary values. The Magnificat and the Beatitudes are, in truth, proclamations and they are related to one another in theological sentiment and in social vision. They turn the accepted social values of their time, and of most times, upside down. The arrogant will be dispersed! (v. 51) The rulers will be thrown down! (v. 52) The lowly will be raised up! (v. 52) The hungry will be filled: the rich emptied out! (v. 53) These are revolutionary lines.

Did Mary, then, know that an entirely new age was coming through the son she was going to bear? Did Mary know that her son's "kingdom without end" (Luke 1:33) would be the reign of righteousness—the righteousness which sets us right with God and right with each other as we submit to the impulses of her son's directing words and his redeeming grace? Did she know that her son's words would cast refashioning fires of equality and justice and love upon the earth, and into societies, and into hearts? And did she know that earthly kingdoms and their proud princes, with their arrogance and mistreatment of their subjects, especially the poor, would come to an end as the kingdom of God infiltrated, undermined, and destroyed them? I personally, of course, do not know how much Mary knew, but she knew a lot and surely sensed the rest.

In Barclay's understanding of it, the Magnificat heralds three revolutions—moral, social, and economic. We may be tempted to think that this view of the Magnificat is far-fetched or "socialistic." On the other hand, it may be that we ourselves are too familiar with the Magnificat in an overly "spiritualized," privatized, and poetical understanding of it. We must not rob such scriptures as the Magnificat, Hannah's Song, and the Beatitudes of the Lord of the social context out of which they sprang and against which they prophesied!

Under the impetus of the Second Vatican Council (and the theologians who prepared it) we are now paying more attention to Mary in her humanity, in her autonomy and personal independence; in the strength of character and the determination of will which this magnificent woman of God displayed in her life.

The Council's theology of Mary is found in section eight of *Lumen gentium*. It follows the Council's treatment of the Church as a pilgrim. Mary was a pilgrim too. In her pilgrim status, she was like the Church and like ourselves. She was one of the redeemed as we are, even if "redeemed in a more exalted fashion." She is the Church's and our own "outstanding model in faith and charity." And she was the handmaid or servant of the Lord, as we are called to be. As a pilgrim and as a servant, she was singular in the manner in which she "co-operated with the will of God by her obedience, faith, hope, and burning love." Assumed into heaven on the completion of her earthly life, "Mary is a sign of certain hope and comfort to the pilgrim people of God." In all of this I see the Council placing Mary before us as our great model of the servant and the pilgrim on the journey that is our life and our faith.

Mary was assumed in glory at the end of her exemplary servant pilgrimage. Question: Are you and I assuming; i.e., taking upon ourselves, the attitudes and the virtues which characterized Mary's pilgrim way so that we, one day, will be assumed into the everlasting glory of heaven? Mary is every Christian's pattern for the pilgrim way, and for the assumption that completes it.

# 667 All Saints

**November 1 / Solemnity**

## MATTHEW 5:1–12A

### Our Heroes

As the Red Army approached Hitler's bunker in Berlin in 1945 he decided to commit suicide. He called his household staff together to say farewell. Those he called were his most faithful servants. He shook each person's hand. Last to receive his handshake was his valet, Heinz Linge. With Hitler about to leave this world, Linge asked, "For whom should we fight on?" Hitler answered, "For the coming man" (Anton Joachimsthaler, *The Last Days of Hitler: The Legends, the Evidence, the Truth,* 1997).

No one knows what Hitler really meant. The phrase "the coming man" is a phrase coined by the German philosopher Frederich Nietzsche. The Nazis borrowed some of their ideology from Nietzsche. Nietzsche, for example, believed that Christianity and democracy were decadent. The one promoted mediocrity, the other promoted the herd. Between them they kept down individuals of genius who were capable of achieving what was great and heroic in themselves and in their nations. If these individuals could be freed from the shackles of Christianity and democracy, they would constitute a new type f man. This was "the coming man" that Nietzsche referred to. He also called him "the superman."

The Second World War was fought between the proponents of two opposite views of the coming man. There was Hitler's Aryan man—now defeated in the Berlin bunker, and his hated enemy's Proletarian man—now triumphant at the bunker's door. In this moment, Hitler may have been pointing his valet to the triumphant enemy at the door; i.e., to the Proletarian man, or he may have been pointing beyond both Fascism and Communism to some as yet unknown superman of the future.

Nietzsche's superman is man at his human best. But, as with the Aryan and the Proletarian models, Nietzsche's man at his human best is an impossibility without democracy and Christianity, without freedom and grace.

Is it not the very dynamics inherent in democracy and Christianity—freedom and grace—that offer man his chance of greatness? of being really man? What do I mean by freedom and grace? I mean my best conscience cooperating with God's gifts and graces. The real superman, the superior person, is man and woman at their moral best. The superior human being is fashioned out of freedom and grace. And that superior person has already appeared on the scene. History has already given us many of these supermen and superwomen. And it will give us many more. We, in the Church, happen to call them the saints.

Unlike the Aryan person and the Proletarian person, limited to one racial strain and one economic philosophy, God wants each of us to be a super person. God wants everyone of all cultures and colors to be saints. God is racially blind, culturally blind, color blind, and gender blind in his love and with his grace. The Gospel's call to holiness is universal: it is for everyone.

If we want to know the way to holiness, to becoming the graced and the superior persons God wishes us to be, we hear it detailed in eight lines in today's Gospel. The way to sanctity is the way of the Beatitudes. Here is summary of how they may be understood:

Holy are you who trust in God and not in worldly power, position and wealth.

Holy are you who are heartbroken over your own sin and the world's suffering.

Holy are you who are self-controlled and God-controlled.

Holy are you who long for righteousness (rightness) and goodness everywhere.

Holy are you who empathize with and forgive others from the bottom of your heart.

Holy are you who serve God and neighbor with the purest of motives.

Holy are you who work for peace and harmony in human and social relationships.

Holy are you who pay the price for your commitment to Christ and his principles.

# 689 The Immaculate Conception of the Blessed Virgin Mary

**December 8 / Solemnity**

## LUKE 1:26–38

### A Necessary Grace

The Immaculate Conception of the Blessed Virgin Mary refers to the special grace by which Mary was preserved from original sin from the first moment of her existence. In that sense she is, in the well-known phrase, "our tainted nature's solitary boast."

Because of original sin, each of us here at the liturgy today was justified before God at our Baptism, some days or weeks after our birth. Such was not the case with Mary. She "began her life possessed of [that] grace" (K. Rahner-H. Vorgrimler, *Theological Dictionary*). She was given this "more exalted" form of redemption because she was destined to be the mother of the Savior. It would be inappropriate for the world's Savior to be born of a woman who was herself conceived and born tainted by sin as the rest of us are. For all of that she is still one of the redeemed as we are.

This gift of Mary's Immaculate Conception was not of her own doing, nor was it a grace intended for her alone. It was, as Pope Pius IX put it, "a singular grace and privilege of Almighty God" given to Mary through the future "merits of Jesus Christ" for the sake of all of us *(Ineffabilis Deus)*. It was a grace won for her—in advance, so to speak—on Calvary and in view of her future role as mother of the Redeemer. For all of that, she was redeemed by Christ, as each one of us is.

Mary's graces and gifts should not be divorced from God's plan of salvation for the human race. All her privileges are from God. All are due to the merits of her Son. All are related, in one way or another, to God's great plan of salvation for us. As the Second Vatican Council notes: "In a wholly singular way [Mary] cooperated by her obedience, faith, hope and burning charity in the Savior's work of restoring supernatural life to souls" (*Lumen gentium*, 61).

In tying Mary's graces and privileges to our needs in salvation, I do not wish to deny Mary her autonomy as an individual human being and an independent agent in regard to her own choices and decisions. Mary's personal greatness is, for me, in the manner in which she corresponded wholeheartedly with God's will, and in the degree to which she cooperated with the graces and the gifts and the privileges given her. I do not see her responses to the angel of the Annunciation as the automatic responses of an innocently unknowing girl, or of a purely passive woman. I do not see her "pre-programmed" in any simplistic or fated sense. Mary's responses are, rather, the instantaneous responses of a woman who, however young in years she may have been, was remarkably mature in the ways of spiritual discernment and quite at home in the company of angels.

Mary must stand as our primary model for the Christian way of life—after, of course, her Son. Her dedication to doing God's will is her outstanding characteristic in the Gospel accounts. When she calls herself the handmaid of the Lord; i.e., the servant of God, there is nothing lacking to it. She expresses that service as the free and complete harmony of her will with God's will. With Mary it is always a matter of "May it be done to me according to your word."

May you and I increase the measure of our own servanthood and service before God and among his people.

# About the Liturgical Institute

The Liturgical Institute, founded in 2000 by His Eminence Francis Cardinal George of Chicago, offers a variety of options for education in Liturgical Studies. A unified, rites-based core curriculum constitutes the foundation of the program, providing integrated and balanced studies toward the advancement of the renewal promoted by the Second Vatican Council. The musical, artistic, and architectural dimensions of worship are given particular emphasis in the curriculum. Institute students are encouraged to participate in its "liturgical heart" of daily Mass and Morning and Evening Prayer. The academic program of the Institute serves a diverse, international student population—laity, religious, and clergy—who are preparing for service in parishes, dioceses, and religious communities. Personalized mentoring is provided in view of each student's ministerial and professional goals. The Institute is housed on the campus of the University of St. Mary of the Lake/Mundelein Seminary, which offers the largest priestly formation program in the United States and is the center of the permanent diaconate and lay ministry training programs of the Archdiocese of Chicago. In addition, the University has the distinction of being the first chartered institution of higher learning in Chicago (1844), and one of only seven pontifical faculties in North America.

For more information about the Liturgical Institute and its programs, contact: usml.edu/liturgicalinstitute. Phone: 847-837-4542. E-mail: litinst@usml.edu.

*Msgr. Reynold Hillenbrand*
*1904-1979*

Monsignor Reynold Hillenbrand, ordained a priest by Cardinal George Mundelein in 1929, was Rector of St. Mary of the Lake Seminary from 1936 to 1944.

He was a leading figure in the liturgical and social action movement in the United States during the 1930s and worked to promote active, intelligent, and informed participation in the Church's liturgy.

He believed that a reconstruction of society would occur as a result of the renewal of the Christian spirit, whose source and center is the liturgy.

Hillenbrand taught that, since the ultimate purpose of Catholic action is to Christianize society, the renewal of the liturgy must undoubtedly play the key role in achieving this goal.

**Hillenbrand Books** strives to reflect the spirit of Monsignor Reynold Hillenbrand's pioneering work by making available innovative and scholarly resources that advance the liturgical and sacramental life of the Church.